# Contents

# Is Ireland

# a

# Third World Country?

The Report of a Conference
held in the Teachers' Club, Dublin
on 20th April 1991,
organised by
the Centre for Research and Documentation, Belfast.

*edited by*

**Thérèse Caherty**
**Andy Storey**
**Mary Gavin**
**Máire Molloy**
**Caitríona Ruane**

First published 1992
by
Beyond the Pale Publications
7 Winetavern Street,
Belfast BT1 1JQ

**British Library Cataloguing-in-Publication Data**
A catalogue record for this book is available from the British Library.

ISBN 0 9514229 2 8

Cover design by Maria Holland.
Photographs by Derek Speirs.
Cartoons by John Byrne.

Printed by
Express Litho Ltd, Belfast

# Notes on Contributors

**BYRNE, John**: Dublin-based cartoonist who has published in Phoenix, Combat Poverty reports and Community Workers' Co-op publications.

**COULTER, Carol**: Journalist working with *The Irish Times.* Founder member of *The Irish Reporter* current affairs magazine.

**CROWLEY, Niall**: Community worker with Dublin Travellers' Education and Development Group. Member of CRD's southern advisory group and Irish Mozambique Solidarity.

**KELLY, Margaret**: Works for the Workers Educational Association. Member of the Links Group and CRD's northern advisory group.

**KELLY, Nuala**: Co-ordinator of Irish Commission for Prisoners Overseas. Member of Board of Trustees of CRD.

**KELLY, Paddy**: Barrister. Belfast-based campaigns officer in Oxfam, Ireland. Member of Nicaragua Support Group and CRD's northern advisory group.

**KIBERD, Declan**: Lecturer in English at University College, Dublin.

**KIRBY, Peadar**: Journalist based in Dublin. Has written extensively on debt and development issues. Authored *Has Ireland A Future?*

**McDONAGH, Kevin**: Columban Father, spent twelve years in Peru. Currently researching MA in Trinity on 'Quest for Hope — contrasting the political theology of Europe and liberation theology of Latin America'.

**MARTIN, Jimmy**: Chairperson of CRD and member of Filipino Irish Group. Member of Joint Solidarity Forum.

**MEANEY, Dympna**: Development educator at National Youth Council of Ireland, until her untimely death in December 1991.

**MUNCK, Ronaldo**: Reader at University of Ulster at Coleraine in Sociology. Writes on Latin America and development studies.

**O'CONNELL, John**: Director of Dublin Travellers' Education and Development Group. Member of Board of Trustees of CRD.

**O'DOWD, Liam**: Senior lecturer in Sociology at Queen's University. Joint author of *Northern Ireland: Between Civil Rights and Civil War* and author of New Introduction to *The Coloniser and the Colonised* by Albert Memmi. Member of the Board of Trustees of CRD.

**O'NEILL, Cathleen**: Community activist. Member of Women's Education and Training Initiative. Tutor in KLEAR Writing Group. Author of *Badly Divided: A Study of Kilmount.*

**O'NEILL, Jim**: Director of Derry Development Education Centre.

**O'PREY, Monina**: Director of Gingerbread Northern Ireland. Member of Community Economic Development and Women's Support Group.

**OSMAN EL TOM, Abdullah**:  Lecturer in Anthropology in St Patrick's College, Maynooth.

**ROLSTON, Bill**: Senior lecturer in Sociology at University of Ulster at Jordanstown, Belfast. Co-author of *The Obair Report.*

**RUANE, Caitríona**: Full-time co-ordinator of Centre for Research and Documentation, Belfast.

**SPEIRS, Derek**: Freelance photojournalist, Report Camera Agency.

**STOREY, Andy**: Economist with Trócaire. Member of CRD's southern advisory group. Member of Irish Critical Studies Forum, Dublin.

**TUCKER, Vincent**: Lecturer in Social Policy at University College, Cork. Co-editor of Co-op Guides.

**WATT, Philip**: Works with NICVA on tenant participation. Member of Community Workers' Co-op, CRD's northern advisory group and Belfast Travellers' Support Group.

# Preface

This book is the result of a conference — *Is Ireland a Third World Country?* — organised by the Centre for Research and Documentation (CRD) which is based in Belfast.

CRD was founded by Irish people who have either worked in Third World countries, or are interested and active in development issues. Many of those involved in CRD returned to Ireland and began to work in solidarity, community and human rights groups. We quickly realised that a lot of problems which Irish communities experienced, for instance, poverty, marginalisation, human rights abuses and inequality, were similar to those encountered in Third World countries, albeit on a different scale.

There were also similarities in the processes through which Irish communities tried to remedy their problems. We felt it would be beneficial for groups in Ireland and the Third World to exchange experiences, information and ideas. A phrase I heard repeatedly while working with groups throughout Ireland was: 'Sure isn't Ireland a Third World country, what are all those people working in Nicaragua and South Africa doing about poverty here?' (Roddy Doyle must also have heard this said – hearing the same question asked in Alan Parker's *The Commitments* made me almost jump out of my chair.)

We decided to run a conference, asking 'Is Ireland a Third World Country?' We wanted workers in community groups, solidarity groups and development agencies to answer that question for themselves. At 10.00 a.m. on April 20 1991, in the Teachers' Club, Dublin, the conference took off. The question was asked and the answers were as various and diverse as those participating. People from practically every county in Ireland, and some from beyond, came and shared their experiences. Many wrote to us congratulating CRD on a job well done and asked when we would be publishing the proceedings — and if we would be organising another such day. Those who missed the day asked to receive the papers.

CRD sees this as one of a number of events, as part of a continuing process. Since April 1991, we have run several events which are a direct result of that conference.

During the West Belfast Community Festival, we ran a debate with a panel arguing for and against the motion 'Ireland is a Third World Country'. We arranged visits to the North for three different groups from the South involved in development education and human rights.

A follow-up conference was organised to take place in Cork in February 1992. Many visitors from Third World countries have supported these initiatives.

The contributions in this book come from a variety of perspectives and experiences and for that reason alone they make for challenging reading. No one believes he or she has the definitive answer but all believe that together we can solve some of the more immediate and pressing problems which confront us. Whatever the view on Ireland's status, there is a general consensus among Irish people that economically all is not as it should be and ordinary people suffer. We need to come together and pool our expertise to create a more equal and participative society.

*Is Ireland a Third World Country?* will be distributed throughout Ireland and a special effort will be made to make it available to our emigrants so that they can work with us in establishing a new Ireland. We welcome your comments, ideas, visits to our centre, criticism and support. And we hope you enjoy this book.

Finally, CRD would like to thank the Northern Ireland Voluntary Trust for financial assistance with this publication. Thanks also to Joe Kelly, Ronnie Fay, Andy Storey, Jimmy Martin, Tony Lavery, Michelle Kelly and Nuala Kelly who helped organise the conference in Dublin. A special thanks to Maura Molloy, Andy Storey, Mary Gavin, Therese Caherty and Caitríona Ruane who spent a lot of time and energy chasing up scripts in order to produce the final product. Thanks also to the contributors and the participants who came from all over Ireland — without them there would have been no conference. John Byrne read through the contributions and came up with an excellent set of much appreciated cartoons. Derek Speirs spent a full day at the conference and produced these wonderful photographs. A special thanks also to Bill Rolston, Mike Tomlinson and Fran Devenney.

**Caitríona Ruane**, *Centre for Research and Documentation*

*Caitríona Ruane and Jimmy Martin, Chairperson of CRD*

# 1. Chairperson's Welcome

*Jimmy Martin*

This is the first major CRD conference in Dublin, so it is great to see so many people here today. I notice people coming from nearly every part of the country, and I appreciate the effort that many of you have made to be here.

I hope you will all enjoy the day. We hope that today will make a contribution to what is a very important debate. We also hope that we all benefit from meeting each other and making contacts through today's discussions.

When people were talking to me before the conference, I was aware that very few people knew much about CRD or what it does. As all of you have been given a copy of the 1988-1991 CRD report, there is no need for me to go into the details – simply to state that we aim to resource groups and individuals working for a just and peaceful society.

Many of us who were involved in setting up CRD worked in Third World countries. The idea of setting up CRD sprung both from questions that arose because of our Third World experiences and because of approaches to work that we encountered there.

Firstly the questions ... many of us had great difficulty when we were asked questions about Ireland — what was the problem in Ireland? Why were the Protestants and Catholics always fighting? And when we came back to Ireland and got involved in solidarity work for the Third World, like me from the Philippines, many questions started to be asked — why were we not interested in change in Ireland but only in the Third World?  These were difficult, but valid, questions. They prompted the start of CRD.

The way CRD was set up was also influenced by models that we had experienced in Third World countries. Many Western research centres are based in universities or far away from the local communities. We knew of centres that were based in the shanty towns, in the slum areas of Third World cities where the work of the centre was linked very closely with the life of the organisations and campaigns in the communities where they were based. It forced the work of the centre to be relevant and to be nourished by the experiences and insights of the people working on the ground, rather than to be academic and abstract.

West Belfast was chosen for the location of CRD; it is an area of severe deprivation; Ballymurphy for example has 87 per cent male unemployment; in the Shankill Road area, we were told on a recent visit, only ten students from a total of ten schools passed the 11-plus this year — that is the exam that children aged 11 must pass if they are to get on to grammar school.

CRD has therefore tried to bring the experience of Third World Research and Documentation Centres to Ireland and apply it in an Irish context.

CRD operates from the definition of development education of the United Nations — 'to enable people to participate in the development of their community, their nation, and the world as a whole. Such participation implies a critical awareness of local, national and international situations based on an understanding of the social, economic and political processes ...' It is 'concerned with issues of human rights, dignity, self-reliance and social justice in both developed and developing countries'.

We see this conference as part of our contribution to development education. We believe in the power of information shared between groups and individuals as they work for change.

Thank you again for coming and I hope that you enjoy the day's proceedings.

# 2. Where in the World?

## *Carol Coulter*

First of all, most of my remarks relate to the South of Ireland, not because I don't attach any importance to the North, but because the southern state is the Irish state, the only one. The state in the North is in fact an extension of the British state, differing from it only in its denial of many of the democratic and civil rights and liberties enjoyed by other British citizens. The southern Irish state is the entity born of the struggle for Irish national independence, and therefore is a post-colonial state.

The 75th anniversary of the Easter Rising - which in fact is today, not two weeks ago - prompted an outburst of soul-searching in the South of Ireland. What was the heritage of that event, and should we celebrate it at all? At official level the embarrassment was palpable, expressed in the government commemoration outside the GPO, which lasted all of 15 minutes. But it was in the media that most of the self-examination took place. It is outside the scope of this paper to examine the treatment of 1916 in the media, but I will take one example to illustrate what I believe to be the dominant ideology in the South of Ireland, by which I mean the Irish state.

A number of history teachers were interviewed on the teaching of history in schools in the *Irish Times* on Tuesday 2nd April last, part of which read:

There may well be some teachers who still teach history in a very old-fashioned way, recounting battles long ago and a succession of rebellions against the ancient foe. Such teachers are reluctant to go public, says Dr. Padraig Hogan of the education department in St. Patrick's College, Maynooth. Whenever research students from the department try to find them they are nowhere to be found. "They may well teach it within the four walls of the classroom but won't say so outside." He points out that in previous decades the teaching of history was used to help to inculcate a love of Irish language, tradition and culture, but it's no longer seen in that way. "There may be some teachers who continue to teach history in an aggressive way but they have been left behind - the status quo has gone somewhere else."

What is striking about these remarks is the ordinariness of the tone - it does not occur to the interviewees that there is anything odd about the fact that 'the status quo' in history teaching is not inculcating a love of Irish language, tradition and culture. The clear implication is that there is no basis for 'recounting battles long ago', that the teaching of history to our children should not embrace the fundamental reality that the independent development of this country was thwarted by its domination by a powerful neighbour for at least five centuries, which inevitably has a bearing on its prospects for development today. This is part of a denial of our colonial past, and an attempt to present our history instead as another variant on a general European experience of competition and wars between nations.

In a pamphlet on this subject I commented on the language of modern political discussion, and the extent to which the relations between Britain and Ireland were described in terms of marital disharmony. James Molyneaux described the relationship between the two countries as 'two nations locked in a loveless marriage which has irretrievably broken down'; Ronan Fanning, the Professor of History in UCD and newspaper columnist, and others talk of 'the bond with Britain'. Inevitably this leads to discussions of the future in the language of the marriage counsellor; we are urged to 'forget the past', to avoid recriminations, to forge a new relationship based on new realities and mutual respect, to embrace 'forgiveness and reconciliation'.

It should not be necessary to point out that a marriage is a contract freely entered into by two partners. Indeed, in law coercion can be a basis for annulment. If commentators persist in using the image of a male-female relationship in discussing Anglo-Irish relations, they could more usefully look to the experience of rape, or indeed, kidnap and multiple rape. This is the appropriate image for the experience of colonialism and imperialism - the forced subjugation of one nation by another, the repeated pillage of the resources of the subjugated nation by the dominating power, the restriction and distortion of its development, the enslavement of its children and their use as cheap labour and cannon-fodder.

To pursue the image further - it often happens that children are born of a rape. If we stay with this metaphor, we can regard the descendents of people brought by the dominating power to live in the subjugated country, often displacing the original inhabitants, as the offspring of the rape. How does a mother relate to them? How do her other children relate to them?

It should not be too fanciful to suggest that all the children are innocent of the crime of their father, that they cannot be made to pay, that they should all be cherished equally. Not, that is, if they don't claim privileges because of their parentage, if they don't seek to dominate over their 'native' siblings, claiming superiority because of the mark of their origin as shown by the colour of their skin - or their religion.

There are other, less metaphorical, ways of illustrating our colonial history, and I will leave them to my colleagues here today. What I want to emphasise is that our history is a history of colonialism, that is where we came from and the political institutions and culture we have today are the product of that experience. It is not possible to begin to change the society in which we live unless we understand its institutions and culture in and through which we work. Many well-meaning people who have sought to change this country have started from the erroneous assumption that our colonial heritage can be relegated to the past. Their achievements through the established political institutions speak for themselves.

The Palestinian writer Edward Said, describing the emergence of nations from imperialist domination, wrote in his Field Day pamphlet, *Nationalism, Colonialism and Literature*:

> There is a sort of dependence between the two sides of the contest, since after all many of the nationalist struggles were led by bourgeoisies that were partly formed and to some extent produced by the colonial power ... these bourgeoisies in effect have often replaced the colonial force with a new class-based and ultimately exploitative force; instead of liberation after decolonisation one simply gets the old colonial structures replicated in new national terms.

James Connolly anticipated this outcome in his prophetic warning that formal political independence in Ireland could lead to no more fundamental change than painting the letter boxes green.

While agreeing with the essence of Said's argument, I would modify it slightly - what one gets after formal political independence is a combination of the old colonial structures with specifically native forms of rule designed to legitimate the new institutions in the eyes of the people, and to draw legitimacy from the traditions of the previous nationalist struggle. However, these forms should not disguise the inherited content of these institutions.

In India, for example, Britain left behind an extensive civil service and an army with no tradition of involvement in politics (unlike former Spanish colonies, who, for example, reflect the place of the army in Spanish society). It also left behind a partitioned country and a population deeply divided along racial and religious lines, whose conflicts, not resolved democratically in the course of the country's emancipation from colonial rule, still tear it apart today.

In Ireland, despite our geographical position in Europe and our membership of the EC, we have a typical neo-colonial economy - debt-ridden, heavily dependent on tourism, an exporter of primary products and of labour. Like other former colonies we face uncompleted processes and unresolved problems, whose continued festering renders them more acute. In the southern state we also live with institutions which are a faithful reflection of their predecessors under British rule. The civil service survived intact, not only in its structures, but in its personnel. The parliamentary system, with its two chambers and undemocratically-elected upper house, the legal system, where even to this day legal precedents set in England are used in Irish courts, not to mention the absurdity of 'republican' judges wearing wigs and gowns, are all inherited.

It is commonly held that the role of the Catholic church in Irish society is a unique feature of post-independence society. But in fact this too has its origins under the latter stages of British rule, when the Catholic church was an important buttress of that rule, a mediator between the rulers and the native population. In return it obtained privileges, of which the best known was the establishment of Maynooth, but which included the accumulation of a large amount of property. It also included a dominant role in education and an important one in health institutions and health policy. This role has survived in the North as well as being extended and consolidated in the South since independence.

After Catholic emancipation the Catholic church, under the patronage of the British state, was able to develop as an extensive conservative network and bulwark against social and political change. Its record on the big social and political upheavals of that time is well-known. When independence came and the British administration was removed, it remained the only established conservative force in the country, and was of vital importance to the emerging new rulers. In using it they were only developing a role already written for it by their imperialist predecessors.

However, it is in the specific forms of our political culture and institutions that we have most in common with other former colonies.

In the time available, I want to deal particularly with political traditions and ideologies which exist in this part of the country, and the present tensions within them.

Those who follow debate in the newspapers will have noticed a great preoccupation in recent years with patronage and so-called 'clientelism'. Indeed, one of the main reasons for the formation of our newest political party, the Progressive Democrats, was opposition to this phenomenon, and prominent figures in Fine Gael, especially those from the heartland of the Dublin middle class, have been shrill in their denunciations of the system according to which voters are more interested in what their public representative can do in the way of small personal favours than in his or her record in moulding legislation.

It is true that for many voters, especially those in rural areas and among the urban poor, their primary concern is what their public representative can do for them, how effectively he or she can mediate between them and the state. His or her legislative record, if it is considered at all, is of secondary importance.

I would argue that this is eminently sensible, based on the accurate perception that very little changes as a result of elections or of which party takes power. Changes come about in this state, not because a party with a radically different programme is elected to government, but because of negotiations outside parliament between the government of the day and the powerful interest groups, be they the church, commercial and business organisations, trade unions or farmers. The results of these negotiations, whether they take place in public or in private, are then ratified by the majority party in the two houses of the parliament.

This form of politics goes back to the compromise which ended British rule over a majority of the country and the subsequent evolution of the state. The Treaty split the nationalist movement and led to a bitter civil war. Its terms were accepted only by a section of the population, indeed, by a minority, if we take the population of the country as a whole. Thus the institutions set up by the Treaty had dubious legitimacy in the eyes of a large section of the population, and were imposed on it by force.

This was shown in the results of the first post-Treaty election, conducted in conditions which would hardly satisfy international criteria of democracy today. They would not have passed the kind of scrutiny to which the last elections in Nicaragua were subjected. The governing party used all the forces of the state to repress its rivals in Sinn Féin, many of whose candidates conducted their campaigns from prison or on the run. Its supporters were harassed, and voters were given the message that their advancement in the new state would not be helped by public support for Sinn Féin. That party contested the election on the basis of the non-recognition of the state and the refusal to participate in its institutions.

In these conditions the governing party obtained 39 per cent of the vote and Sinn Féin obtained 26.7 per cent, with Labour and Independents making up the remainder. This meant that, although the population was war-weary and demoralised, and Sinn Féin under de Valera's leadership offered no alternative platform differing in real terms from their major rival, more than a quarter of the electorate voted not to recognise the new state. It was hardly a recipe for political stability.

Had Sinn Féin remained outside the political system, and become a focus for further dissent, the new state would have remained alien to a large proportion of the electorate. Constant coercion would have been necessary to maintain stability, with the attendant danger of an explosion of discontent into street protest and even armed rebellion. This, of course, is precisely what happened in the North.

But Sinn Féin did not remain outside the political system. As we know, it split and the majority became Fianna Fail on the basis of recognising the state. The minority became increasingly isolated, failing to offer a voice to the diverse kind of dissent which remained.

The process whereby Fianna Fail became the main legitimiser of the new state has been described from the inside by Kevin Boland, former Fianna Fail minister and son of a Fianna Fail minister. (Political dynasties are another feature of post-colonial societies.) 'There was no acceptance of the legitimacy of the Free State, which had been officially characterised ... as a "pretence at democracy",' he wrote in *The Rise and Decline of Fianna Fail.* 'It was merely a question of recognising the *de facto* situation for practical reasons.'

All this changed, however, when Fianna Fail won the election and took over the state. One of its first acts was to draw up its own Constitution, the 1937 Constitution. From this time on, according to Boland, 'there could be no doubt, in the mind of any reasonable person, of the legitimacy of the elected government.' It was Fianna Fail, the representatives of the former dissenters, who put the stamp of legitimacy on it.

Thus the acceptance of the legitimacy of the state by the vast majority of the population of the South was the achievement of Fianna Fail. It was achieved by the systematic integration of key supporters into the mechanics of the state, and the widespread use of patronage, especially in the form of employment in local government and the newly-created state companies, and of state grants for land improvement and private enterprises. As well as programmes of social reform for the urban poor, like the slum clearances and the creation of improved health and education systems.

Anyone who grew up in rural Ireland can testify to the important role of the local TD, especially the Fianna Fail TD, in obtaining employment, state benefits and subventions. This system was also taken for granted by the other parties, though they won elections much more rarely and therefore were less in a position to use it.

Thus was the population bound by a thousand strings of

dependency to the institutions of the state, thereby undermining their doubts about its legitimacy. But these doubts linger on, taking the form of a cavalier attitude towards the law and widespread scepticism towards politics in general. Meanwhile national policy was decided by the careful balancing of the interests of different forces in society, expressed in the extra-parliamentary negotiations which are such a feature of Irish government, and the formalisation of vocational representation in the Senate.

When visiting Colombia a few years ago my Colombian friends were always apologetic when trying to explain their political set-up. There were two main parties, they explained, whose origins lay in different approaches to the residue of Spanish colonialism and who both claimed pride in the national heritage. They had waged a long and bitter civil war, although their programmes were actually very similar. They maintained their support through widespread patronage, jobs throughout the state were determined by party allegiance, the left could make very little impact. Then, they continued, there was also a guerrilla campaign whose origins lay in the disillusionment of the poor and marginalised. In this atmosphere crime and disillusionment were growing. They were always very surprised when I interrupted them to say I recognised all this easily.

An essential part of the legitimation of the state was the construction of an ideology to represent it as the achievement of the struggle for national independence to which a majority of the population was attached. The memory of oppression, of the Famine, of dispossession, of physical and cultural repression, of discrimination and second class citizenship was very real. So the new state and the educators of its children, the Catholic church, worked together to present the new state as the concrete manifestation of this struggle.

The struggle for Irish independence was, according to this new ideology, transformed from the struggle for political and economic independence, for social emancipation for all the people and for the full flowering of a multi-faceted national culture, which made up the many strands of the nationalist movement from the end of the eighteenth century onwards, to become a centuries-long struggle for the realisation of a Catholic and Gaelic state. Essentially partitionist in nature, this ideology presented the narrow, repressive, Catholic, economically backward 26 county state as the realisation of centuries of national struggle.

This new ideology was a false ideology, as it denuded Irish nationalism of its liberationist content and ignored the reality of the outlook of the majority of its leaders. It also totally excluded any role in the future of Ireland for the people living in the North, especially the Protestants. It did pay obeisance to the real national feeling of the population, but only in order to contain it within restrictive confines which would not question the country's real subservience to the major imperialist powers and the *de facto* acceptance of partition. Indeed, its equation of Irish nationalism with Catholicism served to consolidate Unionism in the hearts and minds of the Protestants of the North.

By the 1960s, however, it had served its purpose. The state was regarded as legitimate by the vast majority of the population for practical purposes, whatever their lingering scepticism. The economic imperative was to seek outside investment and open up the Irish economy, particularly to British and American capital.

Then came the explosion of dissent in the North. Nationalist rhetoric was a luxury that could no longer be afforded. It began to be subjected to 'revisionist' critique, and, full of holes as it was, it failed to survive it.

Now the language is all of 'two traditions' and the need to 'reconcile' them, thus retrospectively legitimising partition by presenting it as the legitimate product of the existence on the island of two distinct ethnic, cultural and political groups. There is far less scrutiny of this concept than of the ideology it is attacking. No-one stops to ask — what two traditions? — to look at the real geographical, social, cultural and class composition of Irish people of different religious dominations.

Now those who talk of our colonial past are stigmatised as 'unreconstructed nationalists', somehow responsible for the violence in this country, and dismissed as apologists for that violence. Thus serious debate about the crisis in our country and its origins is prevented.

But unless we face the reality that we have a colonial past, that Ireland is to be found somewhere between the First and the Third worlds, that the examples of other post-colonial countries in the so-called 'Third World', and those formerly of the 'Second' in Eastern Europe who have also had centuries of foreign domination about which I have not the time to speak now, have as much, and more, to teach us as those of our nearer neighbours in Europe, we will not even understand the questions that our history poses, let alone begin to answer them.

*Declan Kiberd, John O'Connell, Liam O'Dowd and Carol Coulter*

# 3. Colonial Dimensions: Settler-Native Mentalities in Global Context

*Liam O'Dowd*

## A complex colonial legacy

Is Ireland a Third World country? The short answer to this question is no — to answer otherwise is to ignore the huge difference in material circumstances between Ireland and most Third World countries. The World Bank, after all, numbers Ireland, North and South, among the 30 richest industrialised economies in the world. Of course, we must ask immediately what such categorisations mean? How credible are they? They tell us little for example about the distribution of wealth within countries and where Ireland might be ranked on a scale which measures internal inequalities. When we recognise that there are many poor people in Ireland and some very rich people in Third World countries we begin to see the question asked at the outset in a rather different light.

Moreover, World Bank measures tell us little about the social and political relationships within and between nation-states. It is the experience of colonial relationships which most strongly reminds us of Irish affinities to Third World countries. There is a pressing need, however, to look again at the complexities of this experience and come to grips with the ambiguous role played by Irish people in global processes of colonization and decolonization. This ambiguity arises from the duality of Ireland's position as part of the old imperial/colonial heartland (incl. N. America) on the one hand, and as a member of the group of colonized countries on the other. Historically, Irish people, Catholic and Protestant, Northerners and Southerners, have been both victims and beneficiaries of the colonial process.

This historical legacy has left its mark on contemporary Ireland. Rather than avoid the issue, we need to explore the surviving colonial dimensions to Irish life and the mentalities associated with them. To what extent, for example, is the Irish Republic a neo-colony, a happy hunting ground for a new economic colonialism with its centre in the corporate headquarters of North American, European and Japanese multinationals? Is the Republic a contributor to neo-colonialism through its membership of the EC or is it the victim of neo-colonialism? How does this structure the country's relationship to the 'third world'? Do the governing institutions and political system of the Republic bear the hallmarks of neo-colonial structures elsewhere?

The recognition of colonial dimensions to Northern Irish society fall between two stools. On the one hand, there are attempts to studiously ignore them for a mixture of often contradictory and ill-thought out reasons. On the other hand, there is evidence of a willingness to embrace a crude identification of Protestants as 'settlers' and Catholics as 'natives', as if these categories were fixed and immutable.

In fact, there may be at least three colonial dimensions to Northern Irish society. Like the South, it may be considered part of a neo-colonial complex. Secondly, it might be suggested that Direct Rule has given administrative colonialism a new lease of life. Certainly, a large section of Protestant opinion sees it in these terms. And finally, there is the question of the contemporary status of 'settler-native' relationships — which is the main focus of this paper.

We must address the various dimensions and nuances of the colonial legacy, therefore, if we are to come to terms with social/political relations within Ireland, and between Ireland, Britain and the wider global context. In this manner we can also come to better inform our political choices.

## Avoidance and denial

Despite being bandied about in popular debate in Northern Ireland, words like colonialism and imperialism are banned from polite political and intellectual discourse in Ireland generally. They raise embarrassing ghosts from the past which haunt the business of creating jobs, promoting multinational investment, revising history, reducing the national debt, restoring law and order and above all containing the Northern Ireland conflict. Of course, there are exceptions. Some writers and dramatists, as well as commentators like Raymond Crotty, Carol Coulter and Declan Kiberd, do produce work which registers the colonial dimension.[1] But this work is often ignored or written off as unreconstructed nationalism or more effectively still as providing moral support to the IRA.

Colonialism is consigned in the conventional wisdom to the distant past or to faraway 'third world' countries where the natives can be impressed occasionally by Ireland's historic anti-colonial credentials. This exercise of evading or denying the colonial legacy is helped by an attempt to escape into a wider European setting. Here, the EC is portrayed as a non-colonial replacement for the old imperial states of western Europe. It is presented as a definitive solution to the old imperial rivalries and as a sign that the process of decolonisation is complete.

Accordingly, the Irish Republic and Northern Ireland's membership of the EC is portrayed as a potential escape route from the colonial legacy into a post-colonial and post-nationalist club. Of course, in this context, Northern Ireland remains the most troublesome reminder of the persisting effects of the colonial legacy. This leads to a denial that there is *any* colonial dimension to the Northern Ireland problem. Alternatively, it is portrayed as a residue, as a problem to be contained, in the hope that it will gradually dissipate over time in the wider Anglo-Irish and European context.

I want to argue here that the evasion and denial of the colonial legacy in Irish life risks consolidating and preserving it. It leads us to misapprehend the nature of Irish society and its place in  the world.

However, colonialism is *not* some magic key which unlocks the secrets of Irish society, it is not the single factor which explains everything else — religion, economic development, gender, religion or sectarianism, for example.

What I am advocating  is the recognition of the colonial *dimensions* to Irish life. This does not mean assuming some one-dimensional model of colonialism against which we should compare the Irish experience. There have been many varieties of colonialism — in a sense each colonial situation has unique aspects. Perhaps the uniqueness of the Irish situation lies in the way in which many varieties and aspects of colonialism are interwoven. We ignore these at our peril — at the risk of mis-understanding ourselves and how we relate to global social change.

In this paper, I wish to discuss just one of the colonial dimensions of Northern Ireland society — the persistence of 'settler' versus 'native' mentalities.  Although, any full analysis of colonialism must also address the other forms of colonialism  mentioned above, the 'settler/native' dimension deserves particular scrutiny. From it derives many of the distinctive features of Northern Ireland in the wider Anglo-Irish context. It also generates much of the intensity and bitterness which has characterised the conflict of the last two decades.

## Self-contained worlds

When I first came to live in Belfast over seventeen years ago, I experienced a sense of what might be termed the 'Saigon syndrome' — that famous image of Americans sipping champagne around their swimming pools as the Viet Cong encircled the city. My situation was more modest, of course.  It was less a case of champagne and swimming pools and more a case of sitting at my typewriter while the bombs went off.

In another sense too, Belfast offered a juxtaposition of hermetically sealed social worlds. Here, it seemed to me at least, was an echo of the self-contained worlds  evoked in colonial literature. The disconnectedness of these worlds was striking. The worlds of republicans and loyalists, working class and middle class nationalists and unionists, free Presbyterians and Catholics, English administrators and even university academics were all juxtaposed but unwilling or unable to acknowledge the structures which linked them together.

As a Southerner in the North, it was clear than in many respects Northern Ireland and the Republic constituted two such worlds. Britain constituted another. More remarkably still, this diversity of social worlds within Northern Ireland was cut across by rigid political and sectarian polarisation. Indeed, they also provided an escape or refuge from the underlying antagonism. Northern Ireland was a conglomeration of social worlds linked only by a shared awareness of a central divide.

Given this type of fractured existence, there seemed to be enormous obstacles in the way of a coherent intellectual analysis of Northern Irish society. Even if this were possible how could people be expected to empathize with those who held views wildly divergent and antagonistic to their own.

## A coherent framework?

Of course people can cope with alot of social schizophrenia. My job was to teach a subject — sociology — which frequently acknowledged this capacity in all societies. Nevertheless, sociology also presumed to advance a holistic understanding of society.

I was faced with students drawn from many, but not all of the social worlds which comprise Northern Ireland. The students in turn were faced with, what was for them a rare if not unknown species — an academic of Southern origins.

I had a more specific problem, however. The courses I taught, the sociology of development studies and of Ireland, North and South, posed in acute form the need to make links between very different social worlds. For many of my students, it seemed difficult to comprehend either Northern Ireland or the island as a whole within a single frame of reference. There was little help for them, either in their direct experience, or in the available literature.

The development studies literature seemed to suggest something else, *i.e.* that widely divergent social worlds could be linked by underlying structural relationships.  Development theorists had developed an analysis which demonstrated the organic links between the worlds of  rich 'developed' and poor 'developing' countries. Much of the writing on development was intellectually, if not intuitively, convincing in arguing that our daily lives were made possible in some respects by exploitation of people in Third World countries.

Here the question of how Ireland as a whole fitted into the global picture seemed relevant.  It raised the possibility of considering North and South within a common framework, while acknowledging  the existence of two states on the island.  Could the study of developing countries and their links with the developed countries tell us something about Ireland and *vice versa*? If it could, then perhaps we were making some progress in transcending the narrow social worlds in which we were all lodged.

Development studies, especially when undertaken by Third World intellectuals made questions of imperialism, colonialism and neo-colonialism central to their analyses. Had this any relevance to how my students or myself could understand the so-called Northern Ireland problem?

I knew the intellectual arguments against colonialist interpretations, *i.e.* that Britain, no longer a colonial power, had no economic, political or strategic interest in remaining in the North, that its presence was subject to the wishes of a democratic majority and that  it played the role of neutral arbiter in an anachronistic squabble.  Yet, the development literature made clear that many colonies did not financially benefit colonising countries especially after World War II.  It also demonstrated that there was no single model of colonialism or of metropole-colony relationship.

Moreover, many who rejected any colonial dimension to the Northern Ireland conflict were willing to recognise  that while it may have been a factor in the past, it was no longer so.  The problem with this analysis was that it seemed to fly in the face of what many of the most active protagonists were actually saying — for them the colonial  past, *e.g.* plantation and settlement, was very much part of the present and of who they were.

Part of the reason for failing to confront the colonial dimension in

Ireland seemed to be a kind of humanistic fear on the part of intellectuals and 'moderates', *i.e.* a fear of further polarising the conflict, of giving moral support to those who allegedly wished to drive the 'settlers' into the sea — people whose roots go back at least 400 years in the North of Ireland — longer than those of many so-called natives.[2] Indeed, a minority of Loyalists were seeking to undermine 'colonial' interpretations by claiming to be the descendents of the ancient pre-Gaelic inhabitants of Ulster.[3] While such attempts may have had dubious intellectual and historical justifications, they registered a keen awareness of 'settler' and 'native' distinctions in popular vocabularies as well as their remarkable durability. To evade or ignore the issue seemed to flying in the face of reality.

**Memmi and settler/native mentalities**

Such convictions were powerfully reinforced when I first read Albert Memmi's book, *The Coloniser and the Colonized* in 1975, and confirmed when I re-read it recently and wrote a new introduction for it.[4] Firstly, here was an Tunisian Jew educated in France writing about the mentalities of colonizer and colonized. He wrote against the background of French withdrawal from Tunisia in the mid-1950s — a situation which could be scarcely more different from Ireland. Yet, the mentalities of the settler and native so powerfully evoked by Memmi seemed to be echoed by the most militant protagonists of the Irish conflict. At first glance, this made the latter appear less anachronistic and more a part of the wider history of twentieth century decolonization.

Secondly, Memmi's analysis spoke directly to the political ineffectiveness and personal dilemmas of moderate humanists and Leftists when faced with such an intractable conflict. His own marginality derived from his dual status as a Jew and a native — distanced from the French colonizers and the Moslem colonized alike, yet linked in different ways to each.

Memmi does not provide us then with a total analysis of colonialism, even if such were possible. As Sartre points out in the original introduction, he tells us about the situation, not the system. Colonialism as a system involves domination — economic, political, cultural and military. It is a set of relationships, not a series of battles and treaties. Memmi's book tells us little about economic, political or military dimensions although he asserts that economic privilege is at the core of the colonial relationship. Despite his title, he does not deal with all types of colonizers and colonized — company officials, agents, civil and military advisers, absentee landlords and multinational executives. He concentrates instead on the 'malignant' relationship – what Sartre termed the 'relentless reciprocity' – which links 'settler-native' mentalities.

The relationship is mutually destructive. Within it the identity of the protagonists is forged, and once forged, is frozen. It did seem that militant loyalists and republicans were caught in such relationship. Ulster Loyalists 'needed' disloyal nationalists to demonstrate their own loyalty. Nationalists for their own part were proud to demonstrate their disloyalty and make it part of their communal identity. Even when the 'natives' gave their consent to a constitutional compromise, their newly proclaimed loyalty was seen as suspect and merely instrumental to their long term goal. Loyalists, on the other hand, demonstrated their own loyalty ostentatiously but it remained profoundly conditional on the motherland not selling them out to their enemies.

Loyalists endlessly demanded reassurance about security and their membership of the United Kingdom. Yet, it seemed that no permanent re-assurance was possible. As the 'natives' revolted, Loyalists refurbished their most durable myth, that of the besieged garrison. The fortress continued to be threatened on several fronts: by the besiegers without, Irish Catholic Nationalists and their sympathisers across the world, by fifth columnists who would compromise with the enemy, and by the inconstancy of a motherland with a history of putting its own interests before those of its most patriotic citizens abroad.

Here, Ulster Protestants build a myth of self-reliance on a sense of entrapment. Fundamental to Loyalists' sense of beleaguerment and self-reliance is their commitment to 'lawful' coercion of those who threaten them. Equally deep-rooted is the republican denial of the lawfulness of this coercion and of the right to resort to arms to overthrow it. Loyalists endlessly call for more guns, soldiers, police, shoot to kill policies, for the elimination or extermination of the terrorists. The militant 'native' for his part mirrors this 'settler' commitment to coercion and, in asserting the merit of 'armed struggle' indulges the 'nostalgia for arms' mentioned by Memmi.

Memmi's discussion of the colonizer's 'usurper's role' or 'Nero complex' also finds an echo in Northern Ireland. Loyalists seek to deny the extent to which their plantation origins rests on usurpation by stressing their improving mission — the way in which they civilised a wild and barbarous land. While the 'native' dwells on dispossession and subsequent oppression, Ulster 'settlers' evoke their own technical and scientific prowess, their more rational forms of religion, their greater entrepreneurial capacity, their greater sense of social discipline, their superior welfare systems, roads and hospitals. Their opponents continue to assert what they wish to deny: that some of these advantages at least have arisen from expropriating or excluding the 'natives'. Moreover, Loyalists have an uneasy sense that their advantages are less dependent on their own efforts than on their links with Britain and the absolute need to maintain them. The very nature of the ties to the motherland make Loyalists question deep down their own myth of self-reliance.

Nationalists, for their part, even where they acknowledge the 'merits' and advantages claimed by Loyalists, see them as rooted in their own exploitation and oppression. For Republicans, they are rooted in the link with Britain. Meanwhile, Nationalists assert that their own Irish Catholic culture is older, superior and more universal, than that which they see as an imposed and self-serving culture of privilege. Spiritual superiority can be reconciled with material inferiority.

Memmi points out that settlers enlarge on their own merits by stressing the demerits of the natives. Loyalists' catalogues of native shortcomings is reminiscent of white South Africans pointing to the demerits of black Africans. Loyalists point to the independent Irish state as a salutary example of what happens when self-determination is ceded to Irish Catholics in a manner which evokes white South African condemnation of the record of Black African states.

While often fixated on their own myth of origin, Loyalists accuse nationalists of a preoccupation with the history and myth of Irish nationhood. Meanwhile, they condemn the Southern state as a

Catholic theocracy and seek to arraign it for its treatment of its Protestant minority, its economic failures, its ingrained anti-Britishness and its role as a haven for terrorist attacks on the North. Black South Africans' assertion that 'their' blacks are better off than those of the independent black states also finds a counterpart in Ireland. The 'demerits' of Northern Nationalists include their lack of gratitude for a standard of living superior to their Southern counterparts. In the cruder stereotypes, the 'natives' are lazy, prone to be over-fertile, to have inferior education and skills and to be supine before a clergy which denies them the freedom of individual conscience.

In Memmi's account, colonizers sometimes try to imagine the colony without the colonized but realise that, without them, the colony would have no meaning. In an analogous sense, Loyalists often seem to imagine an Ulster without Nationalists when they claim to speak for the 'Ulster people'. Moreover, there is little attempt to convert Nationalists politically or religiously — to do so would be to spell the disappearance of the enemy and therefore of oneself. In the process, the 'settler-native' relationship would be no more.

The mutual destructiveness of 'settler-native' mentalities generates an intense mixture of hatred, savagery, idealism and revenge. In distancing themselves from this mixture, many take refuge in evading the colonial dimension, in an endless series of moral condemnations and in the policies of containment pursued by the London and Dublin governments.

There is a powerful moral and humanitarian case to made for containment in the face of spiralling violence. Militarisation, assassinations and bombings reaffirm the tyranny of 'settler-native' mentalities. Containment does not in itself provide an escape, however. Indeed, it risks two possibilities. Firstly, by seeking to confine the conflict militarily to ever smaller geographical areas within Northern Ireland, it risks intensifying it. Secondly, containment provides a means by which the rest of British and Irish society is affected insidiously by the exceptional measures pursued to restore stability to Northern Ireland.

In particular, the ideology of containment is about *techniques* of conflict management and control. The problem is seen to reside among those who are being contained, not among those who are doing the containing. Such an approach is ill-suited to recognising the wider colonial dimension to British and Irish society generally. The imprint of the old centralised colonial structures is still visible in the economic, administrative and political institutions of the Southern state. In Britain, also, many of the institutions of state evoke the history of colonial domination. The race question is a tangible expression of its legacy in British cities.

Both states reflect the limits of decolonisation not least in the way their boundaries were established. In 1921, the new state boundaries of the UK and the Republic were established not by democratic plebiscite but by the balance of power and coercion. In the North, this form of constructing democratic majorities undermined the very legitimacy of the notion of democratic majority itself. Separated at one level, Catholic and Protestants, were linked together at another in ways which consolidated their sense of being 'settlers' and 'natives'.

The marginalisation of Northern Ireland from British politics for nearly 50 years allowed for a form of collective amnesia to develop in Britain over the colonial dimension to the British state. The outbreak of the conflict in Northern Ireland has helped awaken elements of the old colonial mentality in Britain as techniques, developed in suppressing colonial rebellion elsewhere, were dusted off. Anti-Irish racism got a new lease of life.

Ulster Protestants now find themselves the butt of this racism in Britain. Many perceive themselves as being re-colonized at home not just by the administrative structures of Direct Rule but by the Dublin government. Of course, perception of the threat is heavily structured by class as is the renewed sense of beleaguerment in the face of the republican offensive.

Catholics, like Protestants, are confronted, albeit in different ways, with old forms of settler colonialism and revived forms of administrative colonialism. Again, the most bitter interfaces are reflected in the sectarian assassination campaigns and the struggle between the largely Protestant local security forces and young male, working class Catholics.

The effects on the South are rather more subtle. They are reflected in the establishment rush to forget the parentage of the

state and the circumstances surrounding it. This means forgetting also that Northern Ireland was a sibling of the Free State, even if it was one which was officially estranged from birth. New colonial dimensions have emerged however. Just as Irish nationalists were once happy to benefit from some of the opportunities of the old British colonial adventure, the Irish state today seeks to benefit from participating in European structures with a strong neo-colonial dimension.

For Britain and the Republic, and for many in the North in middle class or peaceful areas, containment offers an escape from the colonial legacy, an opportunity to locate the roots of the problem elsewhere in the intransigence of protagonists. Yet, there is a sense in which the protagonists are the real  victims of the colonial dimension. Those who stand aside and assume an air of moral superiority should look to their own complicity in either maintaining old colonial mentalities or in forging new forms of administrative colonialism and neo-colonialism.

The structural connections between different social worlds must be addressed, between the developed and developing worlds, and between the latter and the many social worlds which comprise British and Irish society.

The experience of the last 40 years in both developing and developed countries has demonstrated that just as colonialism is a complex multi-faceted system, decolonization is not a simple unilinear process. Sartre was able to say in 1957 that Memmi's work was a witness to the death throes of colonialism. He was wrong. Even if we take the specific aspects of colonialism addressed by Memmi — the settler-native mentalities, it is clear that some of the most deep-rooted contemporary conflicts — in South Africa and Israel for example — manifest this dimension.

Furthermore, it is important to query the extent to which settler mentalities live on in the U.S., Canada and Australia where history is often understood as beginning with the expropriation and elimination of native populations. There are many forms of settler-native mentality. In Ireland, they are echoed not just in the ideology of Northern Catholics and Protestants, but in the relationship between the settled community and the Travellers. None of these dimensions can be written off as an anachronism against the backdrop of revitalised ethnic-national consciousness, secessionist tendencies and quasi-settler/native confrontations in both Eastern and Western Europe.

To fully excavate the colonial dimensions to Irish society it is also necessary to look for new forms of administrative colonialism and neo-colonialism. These are beyond the scope of this paper. Nevertheless, such interrogations can reveal not only something of the nature of Irish society but of the way in which the colonial dimension continues to colour the relationship between first and third worlds.

It is true that the direct political administration of Third World countries has diminished. Yet, colonial fragments run by native elites are still in place helping to operate a grossly unequal world economic system controlled by what might be termed a neo-colonial complex of the U.S., EC and Japan. Direct intervention in the Third World is frequent — exemplified most recently in the Gulf War. It is worth asking how much has changed since 1910 when Jules Harmand, the French commissaire-general in Indochina observed:

> The basic legitimation of conquest over native peoples is the conviction of our superiority, not merely our mechanical, economic and military superiority, but our moral superiority. Our dignity rests on that quality, and it underlies our right to direct the rest of humanity. Material power is nothing but a means to that end. [5]

Today, 'native peoples' might include the vast majority of the world's population living outside the gilded cage of advanced capitalism. Harmand's statement might serve as a justification for the so-called new world order of the 1990s. It is not far removed from George Bush's modern version of the white man's burden. But at least part of this burden has come to rest with the old Imperial heartlands — in the minds of 'new' settlers, 'natives' and immigrants from the ex-colonies.

Ireland is deeply implicated in all this. It is connected to both 'first' and 'third' worlds. Northern Ireland is less a colonial relic than an emblem of how the colonial dimension has survived. We are in a position to learn from the colonizer and the colonized because, like Memmi, we are both. We must attempt a politics by which we become neither.

## Footnotes

1.  see, for example, Coulter, C. *Ireland: Between First and Third Worlds,* Dublin: Attic Press, 1990; Crotty, R. *Ireland in Crisis: A Study in Capitalist Colonial Undevelopment, T*ralee: Brandon, 1986: Kiberd, D. 'Inventing Irelands', *Crane Bag,* 8(1), 1984.
2.  Frank Wright, in one of the few outstanding books on the 'Troubles' (*Northern Ireland: A Comparative Analysis,* Dublin, Gill & Macmillan, 1987), prefers to speak of citizens and natives on the ethnic frontier. He decries the use of terms like racism, fascism, self-determination and colonialism because they constitute a moral barrier between the student/intellectual and the people found guilty of having the problem. The problem here, however, was that it is ordinary people, not just intellectuals, who distinguish between the innocent and the guilty and who act accordingly. It is they who often speak the rhetoric of settler and native.
3.  See for example Ian Adamson's work: *The Cruithin: The Ancient Kindred,* Newtownards: Nosmada Books, 1974.
4.  Memmi, A. *The Colonizer and the Colonized,* London: Earthscan, 1990, with new introduction by Liam O'Dowd, pp. 27-66.
5.  Cited in H. Alavi and T. Shanin (eds.) *Introduction to the Sociology of "Developing Societies",* London: Macmillan, 1982, p.74.

# 4. Ireland and the Third World: Some Parallels

## *Declan Kiberd*

In the week of the Easter Rising in 1916, the *Irish Times* carried little news of the cataclysmic events occurring just 200 yards from its offices. Its editorial mind was on higher things. 'How many citizens of Dublin have any real knowledge of the work of Shakespeare?' it enquired on Wednesday 27 April, 1916: 'Could any better occasion be afforded than coincidence of enforced domesticity with the poet's tercentenary?' Historians still argue as to whether the penman had his tongue in his cheek.

There was only one problem with that proposal: an Irish youth who studied English literature at the end of the 19th or start of the 20th century found himself reading the story of how he had been banished from his own home. The Irish language was banned from state classrooms (until 1907) and in these classrooms children recited at morning assembly:

> *I thank the goodness and the grace*
> *Which on my birth have smiled;*
> *And made me in these Christian days*
> *A happy English child.*

But, hidden in the classic writings of England lay many subversive potentials, awaiting their moment to enter public consciousness. So, the youth used Shakespeare to explore, to explain and even to justify himself.

For Yeats the failure of Richard the Second was not due to bumbling ineptitude but to a sensitivity and sophistication far superior to the mere administrative efficiency of Bolingbroke. His was a 'Celtic' Shakespeare who loved Richard's doomed complexity and despised the usurper's basely political wiles. For him such a text was, with Arnoldian inflections, the story of England invading Ireland. Edward Dowden and the efficiency-minded literary critics of imperial Britain had worshipped Bolingbroke and belittled Richard; so Yeats now proposed to restore to Shakespeare's texts an openness they once had before the repressions of imperialist psychology closed off their rich potentials. 'Professor Dowden ... lived in Ireland where everything has failed, and he meditated frequently upon the perfection of character which had, he thought, made England successful', he wrote; or again: 'The more I read the worse does the Shakespeare criticism become and Dowden is about the climax of it.' Yeats detected in Shakespeare's texts a recurrent clash between a Richard and a Bolingbroke, a Hamlet and a Claudius: 'a wise man who was blind from very wisdom, and an empty man who thrust him from his place, and saw all that could be seen from very emptiness'. It was this clash which he recreated in Irish terms as the conflict in *On Baile's Strand* between Cuchulain and Conchubor. Contrasting the popular poetry of Ireland, which celebrated defeats, with that of England, which celebrated victories, Yeats made his preference clear. In turning to popular Irish folk tradition for inspiration, he offered the same analysis which, much later in the 20th century, would be made even more famous by such decolonising intellectuals as Frantz Fanon and Amilcar Cabral: 'Every national movement ... has arisen from a study of the common people, who preserve national characteristics more than any other class.'

Even after Yeats's successful completion of this revolution in Shakespearean criticism, there were many muscular critics left in England to complain that 'there is something about Richard the Second which brings out the latent homosexuality in readers'. The imperial mind which had once claimed the Celts as 'feminine' was now downright homophobic.

Yeats was not the only major Irish writer to reinterpret Shakespeare as a bard of decolonisation. In the summer of 1900, the Chief Examiner of Secondary Schools in Ireland wrote a querulous note: 'the answering of a number of candidates showed that they had not used the edition of *The Tempest* prescribed in the programme'. Perhaps the youthful James Joyce was among these dissidents bent on producing a more Celtic Shakespeare. For Joyce the entire works of England's national poet were an ongoing narrative of exile and loss. He even took time off in *Ulysses* to set mock questions for a revised Celtic syllabus.

> Why is the underplot of King Lear in which Edmund figures lifted out of Sidney's *Arcadia* and spatchcocked onto a Celtic legend older than history?

And what is more, unlike most examiners, he answered his own question:

> Because the theme of the false or the usurping or the adulterous brother or all three in one is to Shakespeare what the poor are not, always with him. The note of banishment, banishment from the heart, banishment from home, sounds uninterruptedly from *The Two Gentlemen of Verona* onward till Prospero breaks his staff, buries it certain fathoms in the earth and drowns his book.

Friedrich Engels had complained that the object of British policy in Ireland was to make the natives feel like strangers in their own land; but he had seriously underestimated their capacity to colonise the culture that was used to colonise them.

A rereading of that literature thus began. Newspapers began to complain of the buffoon-like renditions by visiting English actors of Irish parts. Joseph Holloway wrote in his diary that 'music-hall knockabout Irishman would appear a lifelike portrait of the genuine article beside the Captain Macmorris as he was presented, in speech, action and appearance'. Resentment was expressed — and not for the first time — against English texts which misrepresented Irish persons, or which wrote of them as if they would never be in a position to read, understand and challenge them.

The comedy Wilde milked from the spectacle of the upper classes conducting conversations in the presence of servants who are presumed to hear none of the intimate details was his own sly comment on this hidden theme. The idea that the lower orders might store and use the information in future attacks on their rulers never crossed the official mind, any more than the English educators expected Irish students of Shakespeare to treat his texts like captured weapons which might soon be turned back on the enemy. The Irish would use Shakespeare to repudiate those critics who 'produced' him in their syllabi; and, more vitally, they would go on to feed these subversive rereadings back to their masters. Yeats's insistence that the Abbey Theatre tour London, Oxford and Cambridge with its plays, though falsely criticised by touchy nationalists as a provincial's plea for metropolitan blessing at the time, was a wholly radical attempt to unfreeze English theatre from its Victorian torpor and reopen the radical Shakespearean agenda.

Previous attempts at such feedback — Charlotte Brooke's *Preface to the Reliques of Irish Poetry,* for instance — had proved abortive and were, anyway, made only by members of the Ascendancy class anxious to clear its name. Now, however, as most sections of the Irish population had a mastery of English, the traffic could flow in both directions. The Irish, mocked as brainless lyricists, could practise criticism in both the essayistic and creative mode and set themselves up as the brains (as well as the poets) of the United Kingdom. Wilde, for example, took a perverse delight in proclaiming that his own republicanism derived from that of Milton, Blake and Shelley, and he was caustic about attempts by literary critics to write such embarrassing details out of their accounts. In his *Commonplace Book*, kept at Oxford, he wrote: 'To Dissenters we owe in England *Robinson Crusoe, Pilgrim's Progress*, Milton: Matthew Arnold is unjust to them because not to conform to what is established is merely a synonym for progress.'

This rereading of English tradition was accompanied by an initial reading of much that the academic canon suppressed, of the texts from 19th century Americans like Hawthorne and Whitman, who had themselves grappled with the establishment of a republican literature, and of those books beginning to emerge from other decolonising lands in India, Africa or Latin America. There were far fewer of these, of course, and so the Irish knew that they must lead by example; but artists like Yeats and Pearse were always pleased to see the Abbey Theatre as the location in which to produce an Indian play like Tagore's *The Post Office*. There was a growing sense of affinity with other colonised peoples. A radical mind, such as Joyce's, could satirise the mindless complicity of those examinees who studied approved versions of *The Tempest* as a prelude to taking up the white Englishman's burden in the colony:

> They turned into Lower Mount Street. A few steps from the corner a fat, young man, wearing a silk neckcloth, saluted them and stopped.
> –Did you get the results of the exams? he asked. Griffin was plucked. Halpin and O'Flynn are through the home civil. Moonan got fifth place in the Indian. O'Shaughnessy got fourteenth. The Irish fellows in Clark's gave them a feed last night. They all ate curry. His pallid bloated face expressed benevolent malice and, as he had advanced through his tidings of success, his small, fat- encircled eyes vanished out of sight and his weak wheezing voice out of hearing.
> *(A Portrait of the Artist as a Young Man)*

Of course, there was a thinly-veiled aggressiveness about such rereadings, rooted initially in a pivotal sense of hurt; but that kind of mood soon passed as young intellectuals began to notice the equally deforming effects of colonialism on their so-called masters. The Professor of English at Trinity College Dublin, none other than Dowden, had written that the pervasive idea of *The Tempest* was that 'the true freedom of man consists in service' whereas to a lout like Caliban 'service is slavery'. The young Yeats launched many sallies against Trinity in general and Dowden in particular, but by the time he came to write *Autobiographies* anger had given way to pity for a talented 'provincial' who was over-influenced by inferior thinkers and who failed to trust sufficiently in his own nature. The hostility towards books and booklearning throughout *Autobiographies* is not just a way of defending oral tradition but also an expression of Yeats's contempt for the use made of the coloniser's approved books to pass on second-hand opinions. In a similar trajectory through Joyce's *Portrait*, Stephen Dedalus's initial feeling for the Englishman who is Dean of Studies at the National University is 'a smart of dejection that this man to whom he was speaking was a countryman of Ben Jonson's'; but after the Dean has failed to understand the old English word 'tundish', Stephen's final attitude is a 'desolating pity for this faithful serving-man of the knightly Loyola'. By the time he wrote *Ulysses*, Joyce had had many dealings with the rather manic representatives of England overseas and had begun to suspect that the stress on ruling functionaries caused many to go mad.

The 'tundish' incident is a reminder that the colony retains many of the linguistic features of Shakespearean England, words and phrases which have long fallen into disuse in the parent country. Everything in a colony petrifies — laws, fashions, customs — and the coloniser may grow in time to resent the parent country's failure to remain the model it once was. By 1904 Shaw could jocularly proclaim that Ireland — like India — was one of the last spots on earth still producing the ideal Englishman of history. And, Synge might have added, still speaking Shakespeare's English:

> It is probable that when the Elizabethan dramatist took his ink- horn and sat down to his work he used many phrases that he had just heard, as he sat at dinner, from his mother and children. In Ireland those of us who know the people have the same privilege ... In Ireland, for a few years more, we have a popular imagination that is fiery, magnificent and tender; so that those of us who wish to write start with a chance that is not given to writers in places where the springtime of the local life has been forgotten, and the harvest is a memory only, and the straw has been turned into bricks.

It is possible for Seamus Deane to see in such a moment a last-ditch by the Anglo-Irish mind to hold the parent country true to that full-blooded culture which was taken to justify the imperial enterprise; and this was doubtless why Patrick Kavanagh dubbed the revival led by Yeats and Synge 'a thoroughgoing English-bred lie'. However, all nationalist movements must kick-start themselves into being by repeating elements of the opposed imperial culture, but this in no way implies that they intend to repeat its mistakes. It is one thing to imitate your Shakespearean father; it is quite another to follow Yeats's example and turn him into a revised version of yourself. Moreover, both Yeats and Synge were reaching back beyond the imperial mission to a premodern carnivalesque vitality, to those elements shared by all peoples before the fall into colonialism, elements which survived in Shakespeare's plays and which related, in various ways, to the folk traditions of rural Ireland. All that was most subversive in Shakespeare's texts seemed to connect with all in Ireland that remained untouched by the effects of imperial anglicisation. Like the surrealists who later explored the 'Third World' of all those rejected materials driven deep into the subconscious, Irish artists seized upon all that was denied in official

culture — holy wells, pagan feasts, popular lore, and wrought all to high art. The threat to such richness came not just from industrial England but also from the respectability of the emerging Irish middle class ... as Synge diagnosed, anticipating Fanon and Cabral on this point too.

Central to all this was a healthy refusal to play the victim's part, and a generous insistence that the deformities visited by colonialism upon the Irish were as nothing compared to the repressions suffered by the British, rulers as well as ruled. In saving themselves the Irish would also save their erstwhile masters, and ultimately the whole colonial world: by 1914 Lenin had developed the thesis that a rebellion in Ireland 'is of a hundred times greater political significance than a blow of equal weight in Asia or Africa' — and this because, as Marx had said, 'Ireland lost, the British "Empire" is gone, and the class war in England, till now somnolent and chronic, will assume acute forms'.

So it should not seem surprising that Irish writers set themselves the task of dismantling the master narratives of the neighbouring island, or of restoring to them a pristine openness which they once had. In this they had much in common with West Indian writers, such as C.L.R. James, who read Shakespeare's texts as demonstrating that outsiders had been the decisive agents of history and the holders of the keys to changing worlds. Being on the edge, a Shylock or an Othello saw more and deeper than those within society, and from this knowledge learned what kind of creature man truly is. Of no play were more rereadings offered than of *The Tempest*, for this was the master-text which allowed Caliban, whether he was Irish, Trinidadian or indeed proletarian to see, as if for the first time, his own face in a mirror. And the uncertainty as to what sort of creature Caliban is may in this context be part of Shakespeare's point. The conflation by Shakespeare of Brazilians, Bermudans and New Worlders, along with references to Tunis, Algiers and Egypt, reinforce a sense of *The Tempest* as one of the first writings of the Third World.

# 5. Solidarity: A Two-Way Process

*Caitríona Ruane*

Ba mhaith liom fáilte a chur chuig gach duine anseo. Tá áthas orm go bhfuilimid anseo inniú agus tá súil agam go bhfainfimid taitneamh as an tráthnóna.

Joint Solidarity Forum define solidarity in their publication *Third World Now* in the following way:

> We as solidarity groups, must operate out of a clear definition of solidarity. We must examine our practice constantly in the light of this definition. All too often our careless practice can contribute to a confusion about what solidarity really means.
>
> Solidarity is about partnership. The partners share a common and specific vision which is the basis of the solidarity. From this basis flows a practice which is, in essence, the pursuit of common interests. Solidarity is about involvement in a common struggle. This struggle is taking place in both the so-called First World and the so-called Third World.

Irish people for generations have been in solidarity with peoples struggling against colonialism throughout the world. We have always been in empathy with these people struggling for justice and self-determination. We have had in the recent past a Nobel and Lenin peace prizewinner, Séan MacBride, who worked for the oppressed and marginalised at home and abroad until the day he

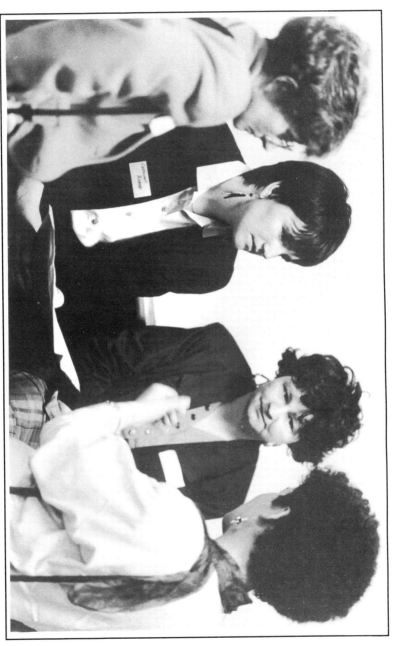

*(from left to right) Paddy Kelly, Caitríona Ruane, Mary Gavin and Nuala Kelly*

died. We supported the freedom of small nations and ethnic groups at many international fora in the past even when it meant incurring the wrath of the imperial powers. Irish women were at the forefront of the suffragette movement. We demonstrated against the war in Vietnam; we march in the streets for the right of Central American people to self determination; we protested against the inhuman Gulf War that we have just witnessed. Ten employees at the Henry Street branch of Dunnes Stores went on strike for over a year and only came off it when the government in the South of Ireland announced it proposed to restrict all imports of South African fruit and vegetables. Our Third World agencies have supported organisations working for change and empowerment of local people in every country in the developing world. People all over Ireland have a genuine concern for people suffering throughout the world and that manifests itself at many different levels of Irish society.

And that solidarity is reciprocal. Countries all over the world looked to Ireland and supported our struggle in many ways and looked at the lessons that could be learned. Peter Beresford Ellis in his book *History of the Irish Working Class* cites the following example:

> On October 25 (1920), Lord Mayor of Cork, Terence MacSwiney — poet, dramatist and scholar — died on the 74th day of a hunger strike while in Brixton Prison, London. A young Vietnamese dishwasher in the Carlton Hotel, London, broke down and cried when he heard the news. "A nation which has such citizens will never surrender." His name was Nguyen Ai Quoc who in 1941 adopted the name of Ho Chi Minh and took lessons of the Irish anti-imperialist fight to his own country.

An Irish person in most countries in the world is made to feel welcome. Certainly in my years in Central America I experienced the warmth of that welcome. As soon as they heard 'Ireland' there was an immediate empathy with me and an acknowledgment of the struggles that Irish people have waged for centuries. I was in India a few years ago on a visit and I remember an old man in the marketplace shaking my hand saying in his broken English 'Sinn

Féin — de Valera' when he heard I was Irish. The main square in Delhi is called Connaught Place in remembrance of the Connaught Rangers who mutinied against the British Army in 1916.

Nehru, the first Prime Minister of India, wrote in his *Glimpses of World History*, which was written in a British jail in India in March 1933:

> This green and beautiful island dips into the Atlantic Ocean on the far west of Europe. It is a small island, lying away from the main currents of world history; but little as it is, it is full of romance, and for centuries past it has shown invincible courage and sacrifice in the struggle for national freedom. Ireland has put up an amazing record of perseverance in this struggle against a powerful neighbour ... it is a brave and irrepressible country and not all the might of the British Empire has been able to crush its spirit or cow it into submission.

The Land League in 1879 was an internationally acclaimed movement. It became such a threat to the British establishment that they denounced it as 'Communism in Connaught'. They claimed it was part of a 'gigantic revolutionary scheme' to unite with 'extreme radicals' in England and labour movements in the U.S. under the banner of revolution. The tactics used by the Land League were studied by movements all over the world.

Last week I watched the epic *Dances with Wolves* about the near annihilation of the native American tribes in the US and thought of the Choctaw tribe. That tribe of Indians heard of the famine in Ireland, they organised a meeting in Skullyville, Oklahoma, and collected $710 (a sizeable amount of money then) for the famine victims in Ireland. Fifteen years previously they themselves had been forcibly removed from their lands in Mississippi to Oklahoma and they lost 14,000 of their people on that 600-mile walk. Last year the chief of the Choctaws, Hollis Roberts, came to Mayo at the invitation of AfrI, to commemorate Irish famine victims and famine victims all over the world.

The reason that all this solidarity and empathy has existed down through the centuries is because there is a recognition by anyone involved in struggling for change that it must be universal change.

They understand that it is the same mechanism all over the world that is the cause of poverty, militarisation and underdevelopment. The superpowers have adapted strategies for different situations. However, upon close examination they are essentially the same, with a few variations.

Sometimes people are surprised when Irish development workers who have worked in Third World countries express concern about the levels of poverty, inequality and marginalisation in Ireland. They argue that there is no comparison between poverty in Ireland and developing countries — that really in comparison to those countries we do not suffer at all. And that begs the question: what is poverty? How do you measure it? Where do you draw the line?

Poverty and inequality are unacceptable wherever they are. Trying to compare poverty with poverty is a futile exercise. It is an insult to anyone living in poverty. Very few Latin American countries have experienced the levels of famine and starvation that Ethiopia and Sudan or the Kurdish people are experiencing now. Does that mean that people in Latin America are not living in poverty? People in Ballymun, Darndale, Creggan, West Belfast and parts of the West of Ireland obviously do not experience the same scale of poverty as many people in developing countries. Try telling a woman trying to eke out a living for her family on unemployment benefit in Ireland not to worry because people in El Salvador are much worse off. I doubt if it will be much consolation to her. This inevitably leads one to a definition of poverty which looks at structures and economic relationships in any given country and asking fundamental questions like: Who are the powerful and wealthy in our society? Who are the marginalised and powerless? What structures are being used to maintain the status quo? In whose interests are they being maintained and what are we going to do about challenging them? Once we have done this analysis I would suggest that our starting point should be to listen to the marginalised and powerless in our society if we are really to understand the extent of alienation and what is needed to bring about social change.

It is a diversion arguing about scales of poverty, a diversion usually created by people who have never suffered hunger or marginalisation. CRD has hosted many Third World visitors over the last three years in Belfast and they have never attempted to compare their situation with ours here in Ireland. They listened, empathised and supported the work of the grass roots groups they met. They stressed the need for alliances between grass roots groups in Ireland and their countries.

We need to have a vision of a world where people have access to health, education, clothing, legal and political rights and actively participate in their societies. To achieve this we need to build alliances and be in solidarity with people struggling for justice and human rights throughout the world. We need to meet each other, analyse together, build common strategies and alliances and work to make our vision a reality.

If we are to be relevant in supporting Third World countries we must also support groups working for structural change in Ireland. It is an utter contradiction supporting justice for Third World countries and doing nothing about the inequality that exists in Ireland today. Equally I would say that groups suffering from poverty and marginalisation here in Ireland have a duty to speak out in favour of their counterparts throughout the world. I am not saying for one minute that we should abandon our solidarity work with Latin America, Africa or Asia. On the contrary, we must intensify it but incorporate into it an analysis  of the structural discrimination that exists here, North and South. By so doing our work will be enriched and more relevant. We only have to look at Derek Spiers' photographic exhibition of the last ten years of his work to see in very vivid images the growing polarisation in Irish society. Derek could go to any country in the developing world and do a similar exhibition showing extreme wealth and  poverty.

CRD was founded in 1988 by a group of Irish people who had worked in Africa, Asia and Latin America, who returned home to Ireland and began working in their local communities. We met community and human rights activists throughout Ireland and they joined the project. We realised that a lot of the problems which these communities encounter of poverty, marginalisation and deprivation had similarities to those experienced in developing countries, albeit on a different scale. There were also similarities in the processes through which local communities tried to alleviate their problems. There was a feeling that poor and marginalised communities in Ireland and the developing world could benefit through exchange of ideas, information and experience. Since 1988 CRD has worked on community issues, networked those with projects throughout Ireland, drawn the parallels with countries in the developing world and facilitated international dialogue on those issues of common concern. You will find a report of the first three years of CRD outlining some of the work we have done in your information pack.

Sometimes people in Ireland can have a romantic view of struggle in faraway lands. They feel that it is easier to take a stand, that the issues are much clearer. Without denigrating or condemning those movements or struggles in any way I would say that any struggle for social change is difficult, full of contradictions, compromise, uncertainty. All of us here know about the everyday contradictions in our own struggles; it is an uphill battle and sometimes it is very tempting to say no more. It would be so much easier to opt out. It is the same for people in Latin America, Africa and Asia.

I remember once I was with a wealthy family in El Salvador. I had just come down from the war zone; for security reasons they had no idea I had been in the war zone. I made some very mild comments about the level of poverty in El Salvador and one member berated me saying: 'In Ireland it is much clearer, you have British troops in your country. It is easier to take a position. Here it is different, we have a few people causing problems. Don't judge our situation by your experience in Ireland.'

And strangely enough those words from that Salvadoran gave me hope. And we need hope, more than anything else we need hope to carry on. However, the greatest hope comes from the spirit of people struggling all over the world. I remember one time I visited a Guatemalan refugee camp in Mexico and spoke with some of the people there. They related to me why they had left Guatemala; many of their villages had been decimated, their leaders disappeared and killed. At the end of the discussion one of the peasants said: 'Despite all that has happened to us, somos el pueblo de la esperanza, we are the people of hope, we have a vision of a better society and we are using everything we have to fulfil that vision.'

We here today are also people of hope; we would not be here if we were not. At times in our everyday struggles our hope is the only thing that keeps us going. We need to see our struggles as part of an overall global fight, the fight against poverty, unemployment, sexism, racism, militarisation, discrimination and war — the fight for a better future for us in a global sense and for our children.

Let us work together to build that vision. Go raibh maith agaibh go léir.

# 6. The Position of Women in Society

## Women in Ireland
### *Dympna Meaney*

The biggest dilemma I had in presentation was in deciding which areas I would highlight. Eventually I decided to abandon the aim of making it comprehensive or tidy and to present issues which have struck me over the years as important to women in Ireland and women in developing countries. I do not represent any group and make no claim to be representative of women in Ireland. I hope that our presentations will help us all to explore some issues relevant to women worldwide using our collective experiences.

There are many areas of similarity between women in Ireland and women in developing countries and I will mention just a few.

1. In both areas women have become more involved in community/political/social/environmental groups. Nuala O Faolain wrote an article recently complaining about the lack of media coverage of community groups around the country, many of whose participants are women. She noted that the real political debate in Ireland is happening in these groups in local halls around local issues *e.g.,* postoffice closures, dumping, and lack of health care. Likewise in developing countries women are organising in urban and rural areas. Some have become internationally recognised, such as the Chipko movement where women forest dwellers hugged the trees to stop them being felled. There are also small local groups

which meet for adult education classes, to be involved in co-operative income generating projects, to organise against rape and wife beating, to improve health services.

2. Women's participation in the paid labour force, both formal and non-formal, has increased. Women in both areas tend to work in jobs that are an extension of their roles as wife and mother and which earn significantly less than traditional male jobs. Women have a double burden: they work outside the home but they also have responsibility inside the home and for children. Multinational corporations (MNCs) in Ireland and the Third World have employed more women than traditional industries and I would suggest that this is possibly because women can be paid less than men, they are less organised workers than men and so are less likely to become involved in unions and that women are more likely to leave after they marry. When the number of jobs in the formal economy decreases women tend to be pushed into the informal sector, which is less well paid and more insecure, or to be made unemployed.

3. In Ireland and in Third World countries, women are involved in the exploitation of other women. This is an area of enormous tension in Ireland because it raises the whole issue of class. Within our present patriarchal system women are part of and supportive of an oppressive system. Women use other women to mind their children, do domestic work and often for very little money. Middle class women benefit from a class system which exploits working class women. And if we take a step back and look at the world situation we see that our standard of living is dependent on Third World countries providing us with cheap goods at the expense of Third World women.

4. Women worldwide bear the brunt of our present economic crisis. In the early 1970s, Third World countries were encouraged to borrow money which is now being repaid, in many cases on terms imposed by First World banks. Amounts to be repaid per year and how this would affect the economy were agreed in what is called a structural adjustment package. This led to removal of food subsidies, health cuts — sounds familiar, doesn't it? And it has had similar effects on Third World countries.

* Increased unemployment pushing women out of the formal and into the informal economy.
* Lower prices for commodities such as tea, coffee, putting pressure on governments to produce more cash crops to make up the money lost. This in turn meant more work for women producing the cash crops and giving her less time to produce food for her family.
* Cuts in subsidies on drinking water, food, health care, education and public transport all contributing to extra pressure on women.

You all know the story for Ireland where the cuts in health, education, social welfare, housing and childcare have created an increased dependence on women's unpaid work. A recent study on poverty indicated that one of the groups most at risk of poverty was women rearing on their own.

5. Women worldwide are denied the right to or are pressurised into making decisions about their own fertility. In Third World countries, where population size is equated with underdevelopment, population regulation can be very coercive. In addition, contraceptives rejected by First World countries have been dumped

on Third World countries. In southern Ireland, abortion is illegal, divorce is unavailable and contraceptives are available to medical card holders in the form of the pill.

6. Another area of similarity between Ireland and developing countries is around the resistance to women's groups/movements. A common objection is that they are divisive in separating men and women. In Third World countries women's groups are accused of being influenced by white women and subject to colonialism. Often they are dismissed as being middle class women reflecting middle class concerns that are irrelevant to working class women. This may be true or it may be an excuse to suppress any resistance. I think there is confusion between resistance to the women's movement and critical thought about the women's movement. Critique around class is vital, albeit painful, if women are to challenge their oppressors. But resistance to the women's movement can be part of that oppression, legitimised by myths which must be challenged *e.g.,* you/they are not ordinary, you/they must be lesbians. One striking difference in the nature of resistance in Third World countries is the emphasis on culture to legitimise oppression of women. Practices which are oppressive to women are often justified in the name of tradition *e.g.,* it is traditional that women are responsible for the sex of their children, or that they are circumcised.

7. Finally I want to mention women's involvement in national liberation movements. Women's experiences of national struggle are as many, varied and complex in Third World countries as in Ireland. The same debates go on about which is the priority — women's equality or national liberation. The women's movement in Ireland has also been painfully divided over the national question. However I feel that it is more appropriate that Margaret explores this issue in depth and not the similarities between here and the developing world. For me, to reflect a significant commitment by southern Irish women to the national question would be inaccurate. The reality is that for most women in the South, indifference, guilt and confusion are the dominant feelings about the North — with a number of exceptions.

All the above help to piece together a picture of women's exclusion from power. Notable gains have been made in the past decade and the struggle continues in many and varied ways. In a series of articles on women in Ireland recently, Nuala O Faolain wrote a piece which I felt reflected the ordinary things women want and the tiredness that many of us feel.

'What do yiz want?' Firstly to live in a world where it isn't in men's power to give it. I believe myself that women want to be happy and as good as they can and to knock a bit of crack out of life and to have someone to hold them at night and something to get up for in the morning and to look after their parents and their children. Not so odd is it? Not so different from men, really, apart from the Ferrari and being chairman of the board. Oh and they'd like to be safe. You'd think that isn't much to hope for. But in fact there is an almost unimaginably difficult and long task ahead of women in trying to make the world deliver this. And as for our colleagues in the struggle — men, the rest of the human race — they think it's still okay to be baffled and innocent and to say 'Sure what's wrong with you? What do you want?'

# Women in the North
*Margaret Kelly*

When I was asked to speak on this issue I felt both excited and concerned. Excited because I see it as an opportunity to discuss issues I've been involved with for quite some time, and concerned because I asked myself 'Who am I representing?' It is the enormous diversity of the women's movement which, for me, has made it so pleasurable to be part of it and it is essential that we recognise and use that diversity. I have therefore chosen to cover issues which I feel are important today, and have done so in the only way that is valid for me, that is from a personal perspective.

The women's movement in the North is involved in a very wide range of issues, which they have approached, in the main, from a feminist perspective and have developed creative and innovative ways of dealing with many of the problems facing women in our society. The role of the women's movement has been vast, certainly in comparision to the number of women involved. I have chosen to focus on one debate, the relationship    between feminism and nationalism. This is not an easy subject for discussion, for on the whole the women's movement ignores it.

Channel 4 recently screened the film *Mother Ireland* as part of a series of censorship - it had been banned when it was first produced. Interestingly, a number of scenes were 'edited' before it was screened. I feel this highlights the sensivity of the debate - would the same level of editorial control have been used if the film had been discussing the relationship between feminism and nationalism but in a different country? Too often we in the women's movement have also edited the debate, rather than have the challenging but dangerous discussions that are needed.

Feminism and nationalism have always sat uneasily together - Irish women in the early part of this century faced exactly the same dilemma as many women in the North today.

In the video Nell McCafferty asked why so many feminists found it comparatively easy to support women in the 'armed struggle' in Third World countries but found it difficult even to discuss the issue in the North. Is it because the struggle is so essentially different in nature, or is it that the closer to home it is the more we see the complexities and tensions which exist, the more difficult it is to see a struggle in 'black and white' terms and the more we realise there are grey areas very much in need of discussion and debate?

Without wishing to label anyone, the following are a number of classifications I have developed to explain some of the different perspectives which exist:

- Women in the republican movement.
- Feminist women involved in the republican movement and also to some extent in the women's movement.
- Feminist women involved in the women's movement, whose personal views are republican but who for many reasons tend not to discuss these within that movement.
- Feminist women in the women's movement.
- Women in nationalist areas whose gut feeling may be nationalist but who choose community issues as their area of political involvement.

- Women in loyalist areas whose gut feelings may be loyalist but who also become involved in community issues.
(There would be quite a lot of contact between these last two groups but it is very rare for the conflict in the North to be discussed.)
- Women involved in unionist politics.

The women's movement in the North has decided to a greater or lesser extent to 'ignore' the conflict. The argument has been that the issue causes divisions and leads to conflict, and fear that it would lead to a schism in the movement. My experience has been that not discussing it has also led to division and that in many ways we are helping to maintain the 'silence' about the North. I think many women have found it much easier to identify themselves as feminists rather than as nationalists.

Nell McCafferty suggested that the national question was a running sore on the body politic of Ireland. I would suggest that it is a running sore for feminism and one that very much needs to be addressed.

## *Workshop Report*

### Women-only Forums

Arising from the complaints of some of those attending the conference, this issue was discussed at the beginning and alos later in the course of the meeting. Some women expressed discomfort at the exclusion of men; others believed in the need for women to be able to work on women's questions without guilt. Some emphasised that it was equally important for men to change their thinking; others expressed the need for both types of forum 'after the revolution'. Other contributors emphasised similar difficulties of talking with confidence and without fear when working against oppression at a national level, that nationalist and women's issues cannot be separated.

## Feminism and Nationalism

Some women were confused by the term 'nationalism' — a rural and Catholic united Ireland, anti-imperialism, republicanism? In the course of the discussion, a definition of nationalism was suggested which was approved by some other contributors: that nationalism involves the freedom to explore and define ourselves in an Irish context.

Women talked of the importance of being involved in change, of the resentment against feminists for not taking up the national issue. Others spoke of the history of women's issues being shelved, and suggested that the women's movement needs to create a forum and to bring other issues into this women's agenda.

## Women and Class

This topic concerned ways in which women can be in conflict with each other. Some warned that there was a danger of conformity on women's issues, that a history of colonisation had encouraged a lack of debate and discussion and that women lacked opportunities to get together for such debate. Some participants spoke of how women's class is defined by the men with whom they are involved, and that women's identity is nowhere.

This led to discussion on the conflict for women as mothers or career women. Some spoke of how contemporary society devalues mothering, others spoke of how the low wages paid to women who look after children continues this exploitation. Women discussed the lack of crèche facilities, particularly in large institutions, absent even for staff in maternity hospitals, and spoke of the need for more community crèches.

Towards the end of the workshop the professional identity of many of the women attending was raised, with the question as to why other women were not present. This led to a discussion as to the need for information, and on the importance of issues such as money, literacy, employment. Women spoke of the need for these issues to be talked about, and that women working as social workers or otherwise should aim to make themselves eventually redundant, to be replaced by people from within the community.

# 7. Racism and Ethnic Minorities

## John O'Connell

This workshop was opened with a brief explanation of the aim, *i.e.* to learn about racism, what it is and how it operates in order to become anti-racist. Since the group was all-white, it was pointed that this provided us with an opportunity to explore critically our own beliefs, attitudes and behaviour patterns which may be racist without the risk of exploiting a black person in the process. All too often in race awareness training white people put black participants in the position of relating their experience of racism. While this may be interesting and challenging it can also reinforce the notion that racism is something out there which has got to do with black people only, that in a society without black people there is no racism, that racism is located within the black community even. It can also shift the responsibility for tackling racism onto black people.

In an all-white group one cannot hide behind a black person and it is possible for us to challenge each other and support each other to take responsibility for our racism and to develop anti-racist strategies.

Analogies were drawn with the process of men addressing sexism and settled people addressing discrimination towards Travellers. Men need to look at masculinity and their own attitudes and behaviour towards women. In mixed groups of men and women exercises designed to raise awareness of sexist language or attitudes were likely to be insulting and hurtful to the women present. In other words, the functioning of the group may itself be sexist. In a men's group on the other hand it is possible for men to take responsibility for their own sexism without exploiting women in the process or needing to teach them. Likewise in mixed meetings of Travellers and settled people there is a danger of focusing on the changes Travellers have to make to become 'acceptable' and settled people either focus on ways they can help Travellers or else wallow in some guilt feelings. Perhaps it would be more useful for settled people to examine critically the settled community and to decide on ways it could change.

The focus of the workshop was therefore the attitudes, beliefs and behaviour of the participants present and the kind of society we live in.

## Trigger Statements

The following statements were used to trigger personal responses to stimulate discussion at the beginning of the workshop:

> Racism is often unconscious.
> Images are not neutral.
> Irish people suffer racism.
> Nice people can be racist.
> Tolerance is the privilege of the powerful.
> White people benefit from racism.
> The English language is part of the problem.
> Irish society is racist.
> Being non-racist is not enough.
> Irish Third World volunteers  follow in the footsteps of the colonial expatriates.
> We are all taught to be racist.
> Racism is a white problem.
> Travellers experience racism.
> Helping is racist.
> We must change.

Each small group of participants were given three of these statements and were asked to give their personal response, stating whether they agreed or disagreed with the statement. The statements certainly provoked discussion, to the extent that some groups got so caught up in the first statement on their list that they never got to the other two. However during the feedback to the full group there was an opportunity for anyone to give a reaction/ response.

What the general discussion quickly revealed was that individuals within the group were at very different levels of understanding and experience of the issue of racism. Some had never given racism any serious consideration until then and wanted to find out about it. A few had studied the topic in depth and were eager to move on to discussing ways of tackling racism. Others had given it some thought but were unclear about terminology and key concepts. The two Travellers in the group spoke of being at the receiving end of racism and gave continuing examples to support their assertions.

Given the composition of the group it seemed best to start with some clarifications and definitions. Before considering how we can be anti-racist it is necessary to examine the meaning of racism. In the opening discussion some people argued that racists by definition could not be 'nice people'. But what if racism is unconscious? Can 'nice men' be sexist? There were also references to different races and racial harmony. But how do we understand 'race'; are there different races or is there only one human race? What do we mean by ethnicity? Is it the same as race? These were some of the questions that needed explanation and clarification.

## Key Concepts

When we speak about racial harmony there is an assumption that people are naturally divided into different races which are biologically as well as culturally distinct from one another. Most people think that this is very obvious and plain common sense. The idea of 'race' is something which emerged in Western Europe in the 16th century. By the 18th century people had begun to think in terms of superior and inferior races. Such thinking is very dangerous as was shown in a horrific way by the Nazi Holocaust which was justified by the ideology of racism.

Subsequently the United Nations Educational, Scientific and Cultural Organisation (UNESCO) undertook a thorough examination of race and produced a number of important conclusions. It stated that 'for all practical social purposes race is not so much a biological phenomenon as a social myth. The myth of "race" has created an enormous amount of human and social damage'.

The UNESCO position views racism as an ideology which categorises individuals as belonging to a group on the basis of some biological characteristics, usually skin colour. But when one considers skin colour it becomes problematic. There are numerous shades of white, yellow, brown and black. One is led to ask what's so significant about skin colour? There is no evidence to show that skin colour is any more significant than other biological characteristics such as height, weight or hair difference; likewise with nose, ear and eye shape and size. Despite the fact that one cannot conclude anything about an individual's personality, intellectual or moral ability from knowing his or her skin colour, people think and act as if it were otherwise. People continue to perceive selectively certain physical differences and falsely attribute to these an unfounded significance, *i.e.* race differences.

This fails to acknowledge that the use of the term 'race' is a social construct. It is important only because people give it importance. The problem is that when people use the term in a 'neutral' way to describe socially a group of people in a given society as belonging together this falls into the racist notions of inferiority and superiority.

> As a way of categorising people, race is based upon delusion because popular ideas about racial classifications lack scientific validity and are moulded by political pressures rather than by evidence of biology.'
> (Banton & Harwood (1978) *The Race Concept* Quoted in *Race In Britain: Continuity and Change* by Charles Husband.)

As an ideology racism has to be explored historically. It is significant that the use of the term 'race' coincided with the colonial expansion of the 16th century. Later, scientific racism developed as a rationalisation of the slave trade. In other words, racism as we know it in Europe has its roots in colonialism and imperialsim. In more recent years the dominant European economy attracted workers of the ex-colonies to fill labour market shortages. However, with economic stagnationm racist explanations were found and black people were blamed for 'taking our jobs'. Throughout this history, the common thread has been the economic need for workers. There has always been a close link between the ideology of racism and the movement of labour. This is still evident in immigration laws, regulations and restrictions placed on migrants, guest workers and access to different types of work.

Even though 'race' is a social myth, racism is very real. Racism is a form of discrimination which involves unjust treatment, unequal relations, negative beliefs and attitudes. The ideology of racism legitimises this discrimination frequently in the loss of white supremacy. Racism is sometimes defined as prejudice plus power. In other words it involves not only preconceived notions and negative stereotypes but is maintained by relations and structures of power. Racism is present when behaviour, structures and institutions result in disadvantage for black and other ethnic minority groups.

The treatment of Travellers in Ireland provides many examples of how racism operates even when the people involved are white. The refusal to recognise their cultural identity, the persistence in ignoring nomadism and vagrancy, the uncritical acceptance of negative thoughts and the widespread systematic acts of discrimination by the more powerful all add up to an Irish form of racism.

## Forms of Racism

Racism may be at an interpersonal level and can involve attitudes and/or behaviour.

But the more serious form is institutionalised racism. This occurs when the day-to-day working of society operates in the interests of the dominant ethnic group and to the disadvantage of other ethnic groups. Therefore because institutional racism operates through a set of routine practices and relationships it is usually invisible to the dominant group (*i.e.* white people or settled people). Institutional racism becomes evident in the statistics on job opportunities, unemployment, educational achievement, income, housing, political representation and health status as shown in infant mortality and life expectancy rates, for instance.

We may have a stereotype of the racist as a very bigoted, violent or obnoxious person. But that is only an extreme form. Racism is often unconscious because it is part of the social fabric and social conditioning. In that way it is all-pervasive, like sexism. That is why we cannot afford to be complacent. Even if we do not ourselves bear negative feelings towards other ethnic groups we may even offend by our ethno-centred behaviour and we may be upholding a society which does discriminate.

Racialism however is conscious. A racialist actually believes in racial differences and in the notion of superiority and inferiority. It involves negative feelings towards others who are seen as from a different race whereas racism need not involve common feelings of prejudice.

## Developing Strategies

What can we do about racism and how can we develop an anti-racist position? The following is a summary of some of the suggestions made:

* Find out more about racism, develop better understanding of the issue, and become more informed.
* Acknowledge our own racism and try to overcome it.
* Condemn racism as something which is wrong.
* Monitor racist incidents.
* Cricitally explore our own language, attitudes, and behaviour.
* Support anti-racist groups.
* Monitor the media and challenge stereotypes.
* Work for anti-racist legislation.
* Recognise the value of other cultures.
* Acknowledge the social contribution of different ethnic groups.
* Support Travellers' rights.
* Question political candidates on the issue.

# 8. Economic Structures

*Andy Storey*

The 26 counties of Ireland emerged from British rule with an economy bearing many of the classic features of colonial status. Industry employed only 13 per cent of the total labour force, and most people depended on agricultural production, either for subsistence or for export to the UK.

In the six counties of the north-east, 35 per cent of the labour force was employed in industry — separation of the new state from this more developed region of the country reinforced the Third World type role which 26 county Ireland would play in the world economy.

Attempts to break out of this underdeveloped position led to the adoption of development strategies which were similar to those of many other Third World countries. From 1930-1950, protective barriers (tariffs, quotas, *etc.*) to keep out foreign imports were erected, behind which it was hoped domestic industry would develop for the local market. This strategy was also adopted by a number of Latin American countries at that time, and later by many of the newly independent countries of Asia and Africa.

Disappointment with the results of this strategy (including its failure to stem emigration) led both Ireland and other Third World countries to shift towards a more outward-oriented approach from the late 1950s onwards. Central to this new approach was a reliance on foreign investment to locate production units in Ireland. Ireland was remarkably successful in attracting such companies by virtue of its tax concessions, proximity to the big European markets, and the relatively cheap availability of educated labour.

In effect, foreign companies came to be relied upon to transplant the industrial base which the country lacked. But as in other Third World situations, these companies did not transfer their key business functions (such as research and development) to Ireland. Instead, they mostly remained relatively low-skill operations, more often assembling products than designing them.

Ireland has thus pursued two main types of industrial strategy; what is crucial about both strategies is that they reflect, both in timing and content, approaches adopted by Third World countries attempting to overcome legacies of backwardness. These strategies were not adopted, at least in the same form or at the same time, by the developed countries of the West. Ireland's developmental reference points are in the Third World rather than the First.

Despite its developmental efforts, Ireland still possesses a weak industrial structure. Foreign companies generate considerable employment, but constitute an inadequate basis for self-sustaining technological advancement in the industrial sector. Domestic companies are predominantly small and unsophisticated. This lack of a sophisticated, integrated industrial sector means that Ireland fulfils a subsidiary and dependent role in the world economy.

Does this make Ireland a Third World country? The use of the term is obviously questionable — a country which is as industrialised as Ireland, albeit within the limits discussed above, is clearly quite different to one which still mainly depends on the export of primary commodities. But Ireland can certainly be described as a peripheral and dependent economy; that position ultimately derives from a colonial legacy which Ireland, like many countries, has been unable to correct.

## *Ronaldo Munck*

In the field of development economics, Ireland is widely recognised as a semi-peripheral country: that is, something not quite like the poor underdeveloped Third World but not either a fully paid-up member of the advanced capitalist countries' club. I believe there are parallels with some Third World processes of development and underdevelopment. There is, of course, the common history of colonialism which leaves a legacy of distorted economic structures even after independence has been achieved. But in Ireland political independence was only gained for 26 counties in the 1920s with six counties remaining under British rule. It is the partition of Ireland as a result of this which creates many other Third World type problems. The result is an economy which is not integrated and where the prospects of organic development are limited. The political effects springing from this denial of basic democratic rights are equally, if not more, important but they are not our main concern here.

Some writers (*e.g.* Kieran Allen, *Is Southern Ireland a Neo-Colony?*) have objected to the above tendency to seek Third World parallels. The so-called dependency theory from which some Irish economists have drawn inspiration is accused of narrow economic nationalism. However, the Latin American dependency theory is much more nuanced than this. Firstly it never denied that development, albeit dependent, could take place.

Secondly, it never argued that nations oppressed other nations without considering internal social divisions. Of course, certain social classes in Ireland have always benefited from colonial and then dependent development.

Thirdly, to view Ireland in terms of dependency theory does not necessarily lead to a simplistic view of the British demon as the source of all problems. Clearly today's economy is dominated by the US, the EC and Japan with Britain at best in the reserve list. In fact, Ireland's dependent role calls for an internationalist development strategy rather than a return to outdated and insufficient nationalist remedies.

If Ireland is a case of dependent development, then how might we achieve a less dependent, more autonomous mode of development? The undoing of partition would seem essential to a more organic development model. Without ignoring the problems of the East European economic model we could advocate increased economic planning as well. But, above all, a great increase in democratic accountability and people's involvement in economic decision-making is called for.

This strategy could be summed up in the need for an all-Ireland Democratic Economic Plan which springs from people's needs rather than the narrow requirements of private profit. Here too Ireland could learn from the Third World where many creative political projects have emerged which take up as one of their key tasks the reform of our distorted anti-people economic structures.

## *Workshop Report*

1. The group discussed points of comparison between Ireland and Third World countries. We acknowledged similarities in certain aspects: such as an underdeveloped industrial base, dependence, reliance on foreign corporations for employment, and the widening gap between rich and poor. On the other hand, our per capita income (which is helped by emigration) places us in the international table with the richer nations. So where does our true position lie?

2. One perspective views Ireland as a post-colonial state, citing historically our economic strategies from 1930-1950 as resembling other emerging yet dependent nations. In this scenario the undoing of partition would lead to a more integrated all-Ireland economy.

3. Other participants felt that this national theory was irrelevant as we are part of an interdependent global economic structure, a part of world capitalism, and specifically aligned with the European trading bloc. Capitalism creates uneven development, creates cores and peripheries within national frontiers as well as between nations.

4. Looking at economics from a less global perspective, we discussed local economics in Ireland, as experienced by communities, urban and rural. The question of generation of wealth was seen as less of a problem than its inequitable distribution. Frustration was expressed at the lack of accountability, and people's involvement in decision-making. Who decides in our society the agenda for development, choosing one and cancelling other options? Must the relationship between communities and central government be on of struggle or dependence? Our preferred model of economic development would take into account people's rather than capital's needs.

# 9. Human Rights

*Nuala Kelly*

In today's workshop I want to raise some general points about the manner in which links have been forged in the work for Irish prisoners overseas and particularly on the Brimingham Six, Guildford Four and Maguire Seven cases, as well as the Winchester Three case. These points reflect the progression from individualised casework to the more collective arena of raising the cases in the international context as abuses of human rights.

## What Are Human Rights?

The promotion and protection of human rights and fundamental freedoms stem directly from the realisation by the international community that:

> Recognition of the inherent dignity and of the equal and inalienable rights of all members of the human family is the foundation of freedom, justice and peace in the world.

The UN Universal Declaration of Human Rights (1948) was the first international statement which systematically listed a range of human rights as a common standard of achievement. Subsequently, respect for human rights became legally binding on over 80 states which became signatories to the 1966 International Treaties. 'These

rights (and obligations) are universal and inviolable so they cannot
in any way be surrendered' — *Pacem in Terris*, (1963). Therefore
neither individual nor collective rights can be surrendered even in
emergency situations. Human rights are extensive and cover legal,
moral, security, social and economic oriented rights and liberty
(civil and political) oriented and basic human rights. Although they
may be different in kind, they are closely linked and must be
promoted simultaneously. Race, gender, sexuality and age as well
as environmental rights are more recent additions to the concept of
rights. It is important to avoid the compartmentalisation of issues
and remember the interconnectedness of all rights.

## Structured Migration

Economic underdevelopment creates millions of displaced
people which in itself is institutionalised violence. It seems that
people have no rights if they have no territory. Refugees, exiles and
emigrants all fall into that category.

One-quarter of our own population is involved in emigration
directly. For some the experience of migration is positive; for many
it is not.

This diaspora cannot be adequately understood without
addressing the issue of the structured movement of labour and the
context of human rights internationally. Population movements
from the peripheral nations of Europe are controlled by political
and legislative decisions made by the powerful industrialised
nations. Whether such peoples are or are not to be the beneficiaries
of wealth, whether they are to be shut out because they are not EC
citizens or are to be let in: such decisions are made on the terms of
those industrialised countries who have the power to define and
control who is a 'desirable' citizen.

## Security and Human Rights

It is commonplace today that immigration is part of the same
ministerial portfolio that deals with terrorism and dangerous drugs.
Many European intergovernmental initiatives aimed initially at
combating terrorism have widened their remit to include policing

immigration and tightening security policy in general, to ensure tighter controls on the freedom of movement of people. The Prevention of Terrorism Act, and its abuse, attempts to perform that function; however while it creates cases like the Birmingham Six, it does not stop terrorism.

It seems that abuses of human rights are greatest in regimes with little or no popular support. However, it has been difficult to get people to accept that these occur in the Western democracies. This became particularly clear in the cases of the Birmingham Six, Guildford Four, Maguire Seven and Winchester Three — Irish people wrongfully imprisoned for periods of 3 to 16 years in Britain because the criminal justice system could not resolve its mistakes.

## Ireland and Human Rights

The Birmingham Six campaign started with families and a few isolated, subsequently scapegoated, individuals. After ten years the media became more interested and campaign groups were established. Initially these groups, at the local and national level, lobbied the Irish and British governments for justice. Some few individuals had lobbied key people internationally. Finally the campaigns focused on international institutions and human rights networks, as they experienced difficulty in resolving miscarriages of justice at the bilateral or domestic level in Britain.

The way in which the campaigns were built actually reflected a growing recognition of the need to pursue human rights on many levels — political, legal, cultural and social — and in various sectors _ religious, trade unionist, community and women's groups. In the last analysis the international human rights community was crucially important through institutions such as the US Human Rights caucus, the UN itself (Kadar Asmal's submission argued not just on the individual cases but on the patterned abuse of Irish migrants in Britain who end up in prison) and, lastly, the Council of Europe.

Although eventually these institutions and standards put pressure on the British state to resolve the cases in some fashion, it is important to note that none of these bodies was able to solve these abuses in itself. Perhaps there is a need for another body, a supranational body particularly within Europe, to which individuals can apply when their rights are being abused. There is a need to look at something which can make compliance with human rights much more enforceable, in a speedier fashion, and not just on paper.

It has been difficult to move these cases into the arena of international human rights. There are many reasons why. Drawing attention to the cultural background, there has been a practice and an acceptance of the belief that if you are Irish you are guilty. This attitude has to be changed otherwise we will continue to get justification for the denial of rights by the state which highlights the paramilitary denial of rights to their victims. The British and Irish Human Rights Project has stated that 'by internationalising human rights issues at the UN, particularly in relation to the Prevention of

Terrorism Act ... the whole weight of experience of the international community can be brought to bear on in this particular instance, the UK government to seek a meaningful (resolution).'

## *Paddy Kelly*

This paper seeks to explore the question "Is Ireland a Third World Country?" by examining human rights, their protection and abuse within a global context. It intends to look at legislation which is applicable to both Ireland and most of the Third World countries: the Charter of the United Nations, the UN Declaration on Human Rights and the two UN Covenants on Economic, Social and Cultural Rights (ESCR) and on Civil and Political Rights (CPR). It is further intended to focus down on the right to life and examine how this right has been infringed by governments.

What are Human Rights? How a state treats its citizens is not for the exclusive determination of that state but is a matter of legitimate concern for the international community. International law protects the rights of individuals against the state and government which exerts power over them. Human rights abuses occur when the state infringes the rights of the citizen.

What is the relationship between human rights abuses and the Third World? It is not coincidental that presssure for international human rights legislation comes largely from the struggle of peoples demanding recognition for their rights, for it is in the suppression of that struggle that human rights abuses become most prevalent. South Africa and Guatemala are cases in point. Despite the ESCR Covenant,Western style democracies have never taken economic and social rights as seriously as political and civil rights.

The UN Declaration and Covenants allow that in times of war or public emergency (objectively verified), threatening the life of the nation, there may derogation from civil and political rights. But no derogation is allowed from some of the protected rights, including the right to life.

A state can be held liable when its agents have directly caused death or when it has acted or omitted to act *e.g.* the exemption of agents of the state from the laws against murder constitutes a violation of the citizen's right to life. Recent history has shown that this right is most commonly and systematically denied by the state in circumstances when governments, democratic or otherwise, are faced with external threat or internal threat or dissent.

The denial of rights, including the right to life, by Western democratic nations rarely enters into the discussion of human rights. Rather there is a tendency to focus on human rights abuses in the Third World to the exclusion of those which may be occurring in the West.

One such example is the question of the denial of human rights by the British government in the North East of Ireland. Amnesty International in its 1988 report into killings by security forces in Northern Ireland stated:

Amnesty International is concerned that some of the killings by the security forces may have resulted  from a delibrate policy at some official level to eliminate, or to permit the elimination of, rather than to arrest, individuals whom they identified as members of armed opposition groups.

The Committee on the Administration of Justice in Belfast has expressed concern that the use of plastic bullets in the North of Ireland,which has resulted in 17 deaths, may have been in breach of the right to life.

On 19th May 1981 Carol Ann Kelly was fatally injured when she was hit on the side of the head by a plastic bullet fired by a British soldier from a jeep. Eye-witnesses said there was no rioting in the immediate area. No-one was ever charged with her murder. Eight children under 15 years have been murdered by plastic bullets in the North of Ireland. In these situations it appears the state has exempted its agents from the law against murder or delibrately failed to enforce it.

If human rights abuses are perceived as the preserve of the Third World, how would a more detailed and exhaustive examination into the abuses of human rights in the North of Ireland stand in comparision to countries like Guatemala or South Africa? Would it only be a question of degree?

## *Workshop Report*

The workshop covered a wide spectrum of arguments and issues. Below are listed some observations expressed by participants.

* Because of media control people do not believe that there is a denial of human rights in Ireland.

* Our starting point must be that there is a denial of human rights.

* Plastic bullets have been used in Toxteth.

* We picket the factory in London where compounds for plastic bullets are made.

* Most people get their information from newspapers, so if there is nothing about human rights abuses between the pages, the reader believes that it does not happen.

* Do people get involved and become active because of personal contact with the issue?

* Poverty is the absence of human rights.

* You often get the answer that if people have human rights they also have responsibilities. Thatcher talked of responsibilities, never rights.

* If you are Irish in Britain, you're guilty. If you are from West Belfast, you're guilty.

* Human rights as an issue is a relatively new concept in Ireland especially in the South.

* Human rights campaigners from the North have given up on getting support from the South and have gone international and have found it more rewarding.

* Need to monitor governments, the state, in relation to abuse of human rights.

* Most people become interested in human rights because a friend has been arrested or they have a gay friend.

* There is often support for certain human rights but maybe not for gay rights.

* There is a progressive mentality in Ireland waiting to be tapped.

* Someone was amazed at the small numbers at this human rights workshop.

* There is a need to recognise that people in the South of Ireland are afraid when it comes to the subject of Northern Ireland.

# 10. Poverty

## *Cathleen O'Neill*

Is Ireland a Third World country? The simple answer to that question is that I do not know. I have never been to the Third World. I cannot find it, I do not know where it is on the map. Perhaps that is because it is a moveable feast, a condition controlled by outside forces — a state or place of permanent poverty and powerlessness, where the individual has little or no say or control over the forces that shape their lives. If so, then I find myself on familiar territory. If I look at the lifestyle of women who live in a Third World situation, I find that I have more in common with them than I do with other Irish women.

Poverty, powerlessness, exploitation and low pay are some of the things that I associate with the Third World. Along with a high incidence of ill health, large families, low educational opportunities and huge exploitation in terms of work. Drugs and prostitution rings are other images that spring to mind when thinking about this issue. These images are contrasted with a backdrop of wealth, privilege and patronage, which is the other extreme in the Third World. The comparison between my life here in Ireland and that of my sister in the Third World becomes clearer and clearer.

The most important similarities between us are the unending grinding daily struggle to feed the family and the way in which we spend ourselves instead of currency to maintain the family.

I live in a sub-culture of poverty. My poverty is hidden, except to those of us who subsist there. My struggle to subsist is compounded by feelings of inadequacy, low self-confidence and poor self-esteem. I am forced to hide my poverty because of the smug complacency of those who deny there is poverty in Ireland. The 'others' who live in the 26th richest nation in the world deny my reality every time they say that no-one goes hungry in Ireland.

I live in an area where people frequently go hungry. Women in my area are forced to add water to the milk for the family breakfast, after they have crumbled up the biscuits in order to hide the fact that there is only one biscuit, not the usual two. They have become expert at cooking offal, rendering it down to provide nutritious meals for the family. This practice takes time, but they have plenty of it, their time management budget has replaced the financial budget. All of their time is spent in application and negotiation with various state agencies looking for supplementary welfare payments — because, despite the common belief of the 'others', it is not possible to live on a social welfare pittance. Ask any of the 1.3 million poor who live on social welfare or low pay.

Fifty-two per cent of people in my area are unemployed and live on social welfare. Yet when they set up home 17 years ago every family had a working head of household and all were in traditional marriages. These people were not responsible for the recessions and changes in technology that put them out of work. They have been failed by those who lack the political will to create viable employment.

Meanwhile life goes on in the sub-culture. Women prop up the egos of spouses who are slowly realising that they will never work again — that their children will never work, have never known work, despite the huge sacrifices made by parents to keep them in school in order to acquire the necessary passport for work or the forced emigration trail.

Many of these families are managed by lone parents, women like me, who feel they prostitute themselves like women in the Third World. They take dirty, dangerous, illegal jobs in order to make money, all the while looking over their shoulders in case they are reported to social welfare. This way of life has a huge impact on the health of many women. Ill health in our area is high — like it is in the Third World. Many women cope by taking drugs, tranquillisers or anti-depressants or sleeping pills. But unlike the illegal drug trade in Third World countries our drug taking is legal, easy, encouraged. In fact our drug taking increases the GNP. It is easier for medical card holders to get a script for tranquillisers than it is to get a tonic or a cough bottle. These items were taken off the list during the recent health cutbacks, along with smear tests and screening tests for breast cancer. Our health service operates a two-tier system, that is reminiscent of a first world/Third World situation.

The question of whether or not Ireland is a Third World country depends very much on where and how you live, and what class you come from. In my view, Ireland is a first world country, rich in material wealth and other resources, availing of huge benefits from the first world. But those benefits sustain Ireland's first world people, ensuring them of power, allowing them to control and exploit the rest of the country.

## *Monina O'Prey*

American economist Andre Frank firmly links the economies of Third World countries into a mass chain of exploitation and dependency created by both global capitalist and colonial systems. He argues that absolute poverty will continue while systems selfishly cater for 'elite groups at the expense of the masses'.

Historically Ireland was caught in the same chain of dependency with Britain — a chain of capitalism and colonialism. Was it able to trigger revolution to effect change 'within' since the time of partition? With the total colonisation of Ireland in the 18th century, Ireland was drained of its livestock and agricultural products — 'One by one, each of our nascent industries was either strangled in its birth or handed over gagged and bound to the jealous custody of rural interest in England, until at last every fountain of wealth was hermetically sealed' (Lord Dufferin, *Irish Emigration and the Nature of the Land of Ireland*).

At the height of the Great Famine (1846-47) Britain did little to ease the situation. No political will existed then nor does it now to ease famine situations — food mountains fester while people perish. In a unique gesture of Third World solidarity at the time of one famine, the Choctow Indians sent relief in the form of money to Ireland — this from a people who only 15 years earlier had lost their homeland and half of their population in their own Trail of Tears walk. They sent relief not because they could afford to but because they understood; Irish people do likewise today; they contribute more to the Third World per capita than any other country; not because they can afford to (an argument often used to suggest that there is only relative poverty in Ireland) but because they understand suffering and oppression . The Irish government, however, received £1,000 million in grants from the EC alone and donated only £34.6 million to the Third World relief programmes.

Ireland's culture was subsumed and its language replaced. An education system mirroring that of the oppressor was imposed and took no cognisance of the needs of the masses, who to this day continue to be excluded from third level education in Ireland. The chain of exploitation is clear — from the travelling landless labourers (the spailpins) who in the time of the famine were almost wiped out because they were too poor to emigrate to the masses of young people leaving Ireland today. Ireland lost one million people during the famine and a further one and a half million to emigration (mainly the U.S.). Has anything changed?

Ireland has shown classic signs of dependency up the 1950s — long after Independence. Its revolution produced 'partial' independence but did little to break the chains of bondage. Its main export was people. After 1958, exports diversified and emigration slowed down. However, employment in traditional industries did not develop. A new dependency developed. Foreign firms (which make up 47 per cent of Irish industry) located here, providing jobs and income. However, these firms maintain their research and development bases at home and take their profits out of Ireland. They locate where incentives are prime (as in Third World countries) and relocate accordingly — a precarious economic basis for a developing country. The cycle of exploitation continues.

The North of Ireland is similar. In the 1950s British industries located there for the purposes of cheap skilled labour. When recession hit, they withdrew. I can think of the BSR firm in Derry, a major employer, which withdrew in the 1960s, leaving an exploited and powerless workforce. Foreign multinationals subsequently replaced British investment until grants and incentives ran out. Derry has come full circle again in that United British Technology has now located on the same site as BSR, and become a major employer and created a new dependency. The recent recession has once again started the process of lay-offs and relocation.

The failure to promote indigenous industry is inexcusable. Only 6 per cent of our land is used for growing food while £12 million worth of potatoes are imported each year. Seventy per cent of Irish farms are classed as non-viable by the EC and therefore receive no grant aid. Only 14 per cent of fish caught in Irish waters are caught by Irish boats. Of that 14 per cent, 80 per cent is caught by the biggest boats which make up 14 per cent of the total fleet.

It must be said that the North has certainly not broken its chain with Britain (metropolis). Powerlessness, poverty, unemployment, sectarianism and lack of equality of opportunity continue to be facts of life for the working class and in particular the Catholic working class which continues to struggle for both a cultural and national identity. Has the rest of Ireland broken the chain of dependency? Forty-seven per cent of foreign industry suggests it has not, as does the cycle of borrowing to bolster the economy. Post- World War II, Ireland borrowed cheaply to rebuild but by the 1970s borrowing (at four times the repayment rate) had emerged as a key element in the economy. The foreign debt per head in Ireland is about twice as high as that of Mexico, Brazil or Argentina, countries whose debt crises have been making world headlines. Ireland is caught in exactly the same cycle of debt and poverty as other Third World countries; as interest rates rise, people either die of starvation or have vital support services curtailed (*e.g.* health, welfare and education). People are dying because of inadequate funding to health services. Third World countries are being strangled by foreign debt — the enrichment of the rich based on the impoverishment of the poor.

In the North, 30-40 per cent of people live on or below the poverty line. In the South, the Combat Poverty Agency estimates that 34 per cent of people are living in poverty (1988). Unemployment is at an all-time high.

In many areas of the North unemployment tops 80 per cent. Underdeveloped regions produce mass poverty and unemployment — another Third World analogy.

It is a fact that the unemployed and their families have considerably worse health both physically and mentally than those in work. A further important issue is that women make up half of the global population; do two thirds of the work; receive one-tenth of the world's income and possess one per cent of the world's property (International Labour Organisation Report). The feminisation of poverty is now a major issue. Poverty affects women more than men. They are paid less, work more and manage on ever decreasing budgets in real terms. They experience inequality of opportunity and are often given the status of dependants. Little recognition is given to particularly marginalised groupings within our society, *e.g.* lone mothers: 45,000 plus lone parent families are headed by women in the North and 70 per cent of these exist on base line benefits. They pay up to 40 per cent more for food and fuel due to regional inequalities than the English claimant receiving exactly the same benefit. Stigma is attached by society to lone parenthood as it is to those who have become known as the undeserving poor — the unemployed, the underclass.

The Thatcher years brought a doubling of the numbers of homeless families and a 50 per cent increase in the number of base line benefit claimants. But the Tory government continues to argue that there is no growth in poverty — 'merely a growth in the poverty industry', *i.e.* organisations campaigning for the poor whose self-interest is served by asserting the widespread nature of the problem. Emigration figures are now soaring throughout Ireland — an estimated 40,000 people leave annually. Almost 50 per cent of them are women. Since partition, an estimated 441,000 have left the North — 263,000 for good, twice as many Catholics as Protestants.

Emigrating by choice is one thing; emigrating for survival is quite another. This has been the case historically in Ireland and now pertains; emigration is linked to poverty. Most emigrants are now heading to Britain. The chain of dependency is strengthening again. The impact of the loss of a middle generation to many impoverished regions should not be ignored. Who is left to question, to work the land, to innovate, to effect change?

> In the years since Independence, Ireland's economy like those of the Third World and post-imperialist nations has had to face and continues to face enormous obstacles to its progress and development. (*Cara Report,* 1986)

In conclusion, it has been suggested that Irish people have forgotten how to ask questions. Is this because of low self-esteem and cultural confusion, linked to poverty and dependency? Is it because our education system teaches us social control and acceptance? Have our civil liberties been so usurped that we cannot see what is in front of us? We are the most policed country in the world — are we beyond revolution? Are our youth being educated for education's sake, trained for training's sake? Is there a new culture of silence? Paulo Freire said: 'Education is never neutral. It is either a force for oppression or liberation.' We have a long way to go — think of this.

> The translation of a need or want into a right is the most widespread and dangerous of modern heresies — Enoch Powell, *Still to Decide*

> Washing our hands of the conflict between the powerful and the powerless means to side with the powerful, not to remain neutral — Paulo Freire

# *Workshop Report*

Is there a problem in comparing Irish to Third World poverty? In one sense, yes there is — nobody is dying of hunger in Ireland. But some people are hungry in Ireland. And we are seeing the emergence of a growing underclass for the same reasons as in the Third World — distorted economic development, debt repayment, *etc*.

This is associated with the de-skilling of much of the workforce and the emergence of monopoly economic power in the hands of a few. The policy response (especially in the North) is to support the 'enterprise culture' rather than community/cooperative schemes which could tackle poverty on the basis of people's own priorities.

In some ways there is less action against poverty in Ireland that there is in the Third World — the underlying causes are perceived to be different while in fact they are similar. To take action you have to start at local level, show the links between different local situations and build relations of solidarity (with Ireland and between Ireland and elsewhere).

Women are disproportionately affected by poverty at both middle class and working class levels which means that some solidarity must also be built between classes.

Practical issues of networking and building solidarity along these lines are more important than asking whether Ireland is, or is not, a Third World country. At the same time there is also a need to introduce more social and political analysis into our education system.

# 11.  The Role of the Church

## The Churches in the North

### *Bill Rolston*

The churches in the North, Protestant and Catholic, are extremely conservative. There are many reasons for that. At the general level, all such large religious institutions tend towards preserving rather than challenging the status quo. More specifically, the history of Ireland, including imperialism, colonialism and neo-colonialism, has led to a specific status quo in the northern part of this partitioned island. The churches have each found ways of peacefully coexisting with the unionist state.

From the time of plantation the Church of Ireland has been the ascendancy church, the establishment at prayer in Ireland. Its dominance was evident in its almost unhindered access to state power which it used to discriminate against all other religious groups. But that is all history, could be the retort. The ascendancy is gone and with it the Church of Ireland's ability to acquire and abuse state power. Despite this, the Church of Ireland wears its confident ascendancy mantle still. It is a bastion of pure old-world Britishness in Ireland, its cathedrals and churches full of Union Jacks, generals' graves and monuments to the wars waged by empire. While the Church of Ireland lives there is indeed a corner of a foreign field that is forever England. There is a veneer of liberalism in the Church of Ireland often absent from the other two main churches. But too much should not be made of that. Often it is a liberalism born of the confidence that a long-standing sense of superiority brings, rather than a commitment to progress in both word and action.

Presbyterians have a dissenting tradition buried deep in their past. In the 18th century they were at the forefront of liberalism, democracy and freedom in Ireland. They still use these words, but the times, like the politics, have changed. Presbyterians overall came to see which side their bread was buttered on and abandoned radicalism for unionism. In this century, if they had been at the forefront of anything it is religious fundamentalism with its paranoia and intolerance. 'Freedom' now is not something to be shared by 'Protestant, Catholic and dissenter', but a tool with which to beat Catholics who are seen as enslaved by an authoritarian, non-biblical church.

The irony is that many Presbyterians, while being the first to accuse Catholic states, such as the South, of being theocracies, would dearly love the North to be a theocracy. It is their view of the world that they would love to impose on all citizens, whether that be sabbatarianism, opposition to gay people, or to abortion. On this score they had more scope when the state was indisputably under unionist control. Their influence over the formation of Northern Ireland's sectarian and segregated education system is a key case in point. Now, with direct rule, they have less ability to directly influence law and social policy. They have still, however, a powerful influence on public mores and public debate, a fact seen most often in relation to matters of sexuality. Nor have they confined their attempts at dictating to citizens solely to the North. Their annual Assemblies frequently condemn the World Council of Churches for its support for movements for national self-determination or social justice in the developing world.

The Catholic church was once outlawed in Ireland. But Cardinal Cullen engineered an historic compromise with the Victorian British government: give us control of a national education system and we will deliver up constitutional rather than revolutionary nationalists. When partition occurred, the Catholic church took a relatively nationalist position and refused to cooperate with the unionist government. In the 1960s an important change occurred. The unionist government of Terence O'Neill conceded increased financial support for Catholic schools in return for the legitimacy conferred on his reformist programme by the new-found friendliness of the Catholic hierarchy.

A quarter of a century later the Catholic church has come a long way. It will never have a direct line into the state, but the hierarchy is wined and dined at Stormont, consulted, and liberally quoted by government ministers. An historic compromise on a scale comparable to that of Cardinal Cullen has taken place, this time under the tutelage of Cardinal Daly. The key to this change is the issue of employment. The Northern Ireland Office has been forced by community pressure to appear to be doing something about the severe economic problems of nationalist areas in particular. In addition, it is believed that high profile economic gimmicks will ensure the isolation of 'terrorists'. Money for 'enterprise initiatives' is thus available on an unprecedented scale. But where money for such areas previously was due as a right, now it is through patronage. The ultimate patron is of course the state. But the state needs a conduit into the working class nationalist ghetto. And the church has come to be that conduit. The advantage to the state is clear. The advantage to the church is that, as church attendance falls and institutional legitimacy declines, it can attempt to buy legitimacy through its high-profile sponsorship of enterprise schemes. And once again the Catholic church plays a key role in attempting to deliver constitutional rather than revolutionary nationalists.

At first glance it might seem praiseworthy that the Catholic church, for so long totally oblivious to such worldly concerns as unemployment, is now involved in promoting enterprise. There are some who might even mistake this for liberation theology. But it is nothing of the sort. Liberation theology usually involves its proponents in confronting the state, usually at great personal risk, over issues of social justice. There is no such risk for the Catholic church. The money committed to enterprise is not its own, the criticism of the state, if any, is mild and gentlemanly. The Catholic church is more a part of the status quo than it has ever been.

# The Role of Church in Society

## *Kevin McDonagh*

It is imperative to state at the outset that when speaking of the Peruvian church, or the Irish church, I am not speaking of a monolithic and uniform reality. There are many different models. Given this context and present time constraints I will limit myself to a brief sketch of some of the characteristics of the 'liberation' model of the church in Lima in contrast with those of the 'institution' or 'pyramid' model of the church operating in Ireland.

The primary challenge facing Western churches is being voiced by the non-believer. D. Bonhoeffer encapsulated the challenge thus: 'How are we to talk of God in a world come of age?'

In contrast the interlocutors of Latin American Christianity are the 'nonpersons', the humans not considered human by the dominant social order. G. Gutierrez encapsulates these challenges thus: 'How are we to tell people who are scarcely human that God is love and that God's love makes us one family?'

How are these questions to be faced up to? The tendency in the Irish church is to refuse to dialogue with the questions raised by the modern secularised and scientifically-minded non-believer. Although the number of actual non-believers in Ireland may be small yet the doubts raised by the modern non-believer are everywhere pressing in upon our traditionally religious ethos. In refusing to face up to the challenge of pluralism and relativism Irish church bishops and clergy tend to seek refuge in peripheral questions of devotions, liturgical reforms and in focusing on the guilt-provoking questions of sexual morality. It lacks an adequate social analysis and hence fails for the most part to speak with any political and prophetic insight on questions such as violence, racism, sexism and the situation of the chronically poor.

The Peruvian church, on the other hand, faces the challenge of the 'non-person', *i.e.* the poor who are erupting in increasing numbers onto the frontline of the march of history in Latin

America. The traditional segment of the church endeavours to reach out to them with traditional aid programmes and paternalistic forms of alms-giving on the one hand, while on the other it tries to browbeat them regarding the evils of revolution and communism. Meanwhile the liberationist segment of the church endeavours to be one born of the aspirations of the poor for full liberation and social justice. The poor are seen as having the right to be subjects of their own destiny and are encouraged and enabled to build community and to act politically for real structural change in society. The liberationist segment of the church takes up a political stance in favour of the poor and oppressed.

Central to this model of the church is an adequate social analysis starting from the perspective of the poor, who are seen in 'classist' terms and as victims of an unjust socio-economic order.

Broadly the Southern Irish church may be described as an 'institution' or 'society' model. This model sees the world as a rival, to be competed against. Its chief function is to safeguard doctrine, promote obedience and guarantee an eternal reward after death to those who are obedient and faithful. In this model the laity usually have a passive, subordinate role, while the clergy exercise leadership through divine authority.

By contrast the 'liberation' model is perceived as the locus of God's liberative presence. It is in the world that men and women must realise themselves and, inspired by the Creator God, humankind has the task of liberating both themselves and creation. In this model of the church the virtues promoted are sacrifice and solidarity, justice and hope. The laity are regarded as subjects of their own destiny and co-workers with God in shaping a new creation.

## Positive and Negative Traits

### *Irish Church*

Church 'for' the people but not church 'of' the people.

Of the three aspects of Christ's messianic 'charism' — Priest, Prophet and King — the Irish church in its leadership neglects the prophetic dimension, *i.e.* the announcing of truth, the defence of the voiceless and the denunciation of exploitation and injustice.

With regard to violence and racial, ethnic and class conflict the clergy hierarchy have nothing to offer beyond moralistic condemnations.

No serious efforts to interpret the theological principle of God's 'preferential option for the poor' for the Irish context.

Unself-critical, self righteous and sexist.

Naive acceptance of the myth of progress, the market system and liberal capitalism.

Signs of a new perspective in recent years coming from groups such as the Conference of Major Religious Superiors and some lay groups involved with the Travellers, the homeless, women's movement and the victims of the system.

## *Liberation Church*

Church of the people and not just 'for' the people.

Large numbers of lay leaders and lay ministers.

Church is a project, a process and not some monolithic superstructure.

Essential link with the popular movement. It is considered not possible to be a 'church person' without commitment to popular organisations promoting justice and structural change in favour of the exploited classes.

Espousal of social analysis from the perspective of the poor. Primacy of praxis over theory.

No private reconciliation with God without commitment to social reconciliation.

On the negative side, this model of the church sometimes does not extend its focus sufficiently beyond socio-economic exploitation.

# 12. Local Communities and Power

*Niall Crowley*
*Philip Watt*

## Introduction

When we talk about power we are talking about access to decision making. This access will largely be determined by economic factors. However, superimposed on the economic roots of powerlessness there is a series of political roots.

Political structures are created to organise society. These structures can fulfil an empowering function or a control function. Economic factors will determine which. Economic structures that enrich a minority and impoverish the majority will require political structures that fulfil a control function. Sexism, racism and sectarianism are also used to structurally exclude specific groups within local communities from access to power and decision making.

This paper will examine the economic and political structures which exclude local communities from power in Ireland, North and South, and will seek to draw parallels with the political economy and experience of local communities in Mozambique.

## Economic Structures

Both parts of Ireland are amongst the poorest regions of the European Community, with lower levels of output and consumption per inhabitant plus higher rates of unemployment and emigration. The economic policies pursued by the Irish government and the British government (in the North) reflect the new right economic consensus of monetarism, supply side economics and fiscal restraint. This is reflected in policies of less government regulation, less 'welfare' in order to end the so-called 'dependency on the state', and shifting the burden of taxation from the rich to the poor. The policies of full employment espoused in the 1960s have now been replaced by policies primarily concerned at reducing inflation and cutting back on public expenditure especially on services such as health and education.

Thus in some ways, the North and South of Ireland, are quite similar; however, in others they are very different, for example in the area of debt and trade balances.

The South has experienced a massive debt crisis since the late 1970s arising out of its necessity to finance public expenditure from its own resources. Its ability to support a large government sector depends on the strength of its economic base, *i.e.* its export industries. Northern Ireland by contrast is a dependent economy whose public expenditure depends not on its economic base but on the willingness of Britain to foot the bill. The result is that the South is caught in a debt trap of Third World proportions. Enormous borrowings and the repatriation of millions of pounds of profits by multinationals has resulted in the South sinking ever deeper into the red just in order to service the original debt. The northern economy remains dependent on Britain, with those who are employed increasingly concentrated in the service sector — or else in controlling other people — rather than manufacturing and industry.

There are parallel issues in the Mozambican economy. Mozambique is in debt particularly to the IMF and World Bank. Much of this debt was casued by the destabilization of the economy by the overt and covert military and economic actions of South Africa. Over 50% of current expenditure is spent against South African-backed destabilization. The result is that, like the South of Ireland, Mozambique has had to drastically reduce spending on health, education and food subsidies in order to service their debt. In Mozambique the debt crisis has allowed the ex-colonial power,

Portugal, to reassert its power through securing majority shareholding in most Mozambican companies, in return for some restructuring of their debt. Although this has parallels with Ireland's former colonial dependence on Britain, this picture is somewhat amended now as the South is exporting to a much wider range of countries particularly in the EC. In the North, the state continues to be ruled as a colony but it is no longer the great economic asset to Britain that it once was. However, the North, like the South, continues to provide cheap skilled and unskilled labour to Britain in the form of the thousands of people who emigrated during the 1980s as a direct result of this colonialism and colonial legacy.

## Economic Structures and Local Communities

Whatever indicators are used, Ireland is one of the poorest regions in Europe. An estimated 27% of people in the North are living in households on below 50% of average income. This figure is 20% in the South.

There are further economic inequalities within local communities. Studies show that women are more likely than men to be poor. Women predominate among the low paid, part-time workers and at the bottom of organisational hierarchies. Ireland North and South has amongst the worst maternity and child-care rights and facilities in Europe. Being poor means that many women are marginalised by both lack of money and lack of time which makes it all the more remarkable that most community-based organisations seem to be run and organised by women working in a voluntary capacity.

Travellers are another group which experience further economic inequalities within local communities. Many local authorities actively prevent Travellers from engaging in economic activity, such as scrap dealing, while at the same time Travellers are discriminated against by employers and singled out for harassment by social security officials.

In the North, institutional sectarianism is as persistent as it was 20 years ago. According to a recent independent report, the Catholic male unemployment rate is 2.5 times that of Protestant males.

Despite reforming legislation, structural discrimination continues to ensure that the nationalist community is excluded from employment and the most powerful positions within business and government.

In Mozambique, the South African-backed Mozambique National Resistance (MNR) terrorized many peasants off their lands. The result has been an estimated 600,000 deaths, 1.7 million refugees and a dramatic rise in chronic poverty. Frelimo, the ruling party, have no longer the finances to sustain many of the development projects in education and health which were so successful in the 1970s. Huge increases in food prices and unemployment are evidence of the harsh realities of the new economic policies forced upon the ruling party by the consequences of this economic destabilization.

Economic structures which seek to preserve structural inequalities will require a parallel political system. The political structure of Ireland and Mozambique have to be understood in the context of colonialism and the colonial legacy.

**Colonialism**

Colonialism involved the extraction of wealth from the colonized nation to the colonizer nation. In Mozambique, for example, Portuguese colonialism was violent and involved the use of forced labour and forced cash crop cultivation. In Ireland it involved blocking economic development to secure the use of Irish labour, particularly through emigration. Colonial political structures involved very overt and tight control functions. In Mozambique elections did not figure in a system run entirely by Portuguese bureaucrats. In Ireland a variety of techniques were used by the British including an extremely restricted franchise, and the corruption of Irish politicians and administrators. Whatever the form, power rested with the administrators and law and order was the central task.

Independence was gained for the South of Ireland at the cost of partition. Partition has distorted the political process whereby power struggles tend to based on the national question rather than class interests. The North continued to be ruled on a largely colonial model whereas the South opted for capitalist development and the British model of representative democracy.

## Representative Democracy

Representative democracy in the South rests on different interests organising as political partiers with elections every five years. The reality of the system for many local communities is great alienation from the political structures.

A number of factors stand out in this system: the highly centralised nature of the state, the power held by civil servants and the lack of any meaningful role for the voluntary sector. Nowhere was this more evident than in the sham of the establishment of seven regional bodies in 1988 to advise on a national plan for the distribution of EC structural funds. The national plan was submitted to the EC before these regional bodies had a chance to even comment!

If we are talking about democracy at national level, we must put it in global context. Many of the key policy decisions are made by multinationals, the International Monetary Fund and the EC. For example, the IMF would only sponsor the economic restructuring of Mozambique after the government agreed to change their constitution towards western-style representative democracy, at the expense of the democratic structures already developed. However, another possible model of political structure is participatory democracy.

## Participatory Democracy

Participatory democracy promotes collective forms of organisation and collective rights with participation as a key principle. They offer a challenging alternative to western structures not only in terms of political process but also in their insistence that democracy cannot be confined to the political sphere but must be rooted in the manner in which the economy itself is structured. However it can be difficult to compare participatory democracy with representative democracy since most examples are countries seeking to develop such a model under external aggression. Overt and covert military or political action has resulted in the destabilization of such models in Chile, Mozambique, Angola, Nicaragua and Grenada. Covert economic attacks have also been employed against such countries by the IMF and multinationals. In Mozambique, the Frelimo government succeeded in building representative institutions which operated in a participatory way at local provincial and national levels. Local communities were broadly consulted on all major issues and democratic structures entered the courts, schools and workplaces.

## Community Organisation

There are other implications for community-based groups working for change that go beyond a position of powerlessness. In Ireland we tend to base our organisations on models we know and dislike! Models of management boards tend to be borrowed from the business world which tend to promote control rather than co-operation. These models are clearly contradictory in pursuing the aims of empowerment and partnership. New models of organisation need to be developed that better reflect the political values we wish to pursue.

However such models must be put in the context of a more democratic political structure.

## Community Work Responses

The role of community work must be firstly to adopt an analysis of society based on its power relationships and secondly, to seek the restructuring and redistribution of power and resources on a more equitable basis. The process is as important as the aims. Alliances need to be made with marginalised and excluded groups, and the aim must be to strive towards more participative structures at local and national level. Strategies must be adopted to confront racism, sexism and other forms of discrimination.

In the North of Ireland, community work operates in the climate where individuals and local communities which challenge state policies are often labelled as being subversive and consequently marginalised and isolated. Indeed the state has been quite effective in devising strategies for the control of community work to serve its own agenda. This must be recognised in the development of community work policy and practice, and all forms of political vetting have to be challenged.

Community workers must also challenge and be challenged on their role in a local community on issues of whether their work is empowering or ultimately controlling. There may also be the tendency to work solely on 'winnable' issues which means that gross inequalities can become legitimized by default over a period of time. Another possible response to powerlessness is solidarity with Third World countries.

## Roles of Solidarity

Solidarity work can play a number of different roles. Information and its dissemination is usually a central task in such work. Developing actions and activities that put pressure on the source of the problem with the Third World is another function. For example, at a local level settled people in solidarity with Travellers have a clear role to play in challenging racist institutions. However all too often the temptation to focus our activities on the Travellers is too great and we avoid the more personally challenging role of addressing the source of the problems faced by the Travellers.

Another role for solidarity work is also in providing concrete resources to support the struggles of those we are in solidarity with. This can be in the form of personnel or material aid. The terms on which this is provided should be continually evaluated - all too often such resources become a source of control rather than empowerment of those who are in struggle. Networking too should be a feature of solidarity, with links being made between different groups pursuing similar struggles and work being done to break the sometimes artificial barriers that divide oppressed groups.

## Principles of Solidarity

Solidarity is a partnership relationship. It is based on a common vision of what is required and a common analysis of what the obstacles are. It is a process of common struggle to remove obstacles and to build the vision. All too often solidarity with the Third World has ignored the dimension of common struggle. The failure to link Third World struggles to local Irish struggles becomes a contradiction. It is also a flaw because both sets of struggles fail to benefit from shared experience and from taking solidarity actions in support of each other.

Partnership is a central notion in solidarity, although this must be partnership of equals. Partnership implies clear channels of dialogue between partners that allow those who are powerless and oppressed to set the agenda of those that are in solidarity with them. It also implies some sense of accountability to the oppressed group on whose behalf a solidarity position is being taken.

## *Workshop Report*

### Problems

Many men are being left behind in the development of local communities, especially those who are losing their confidence as a result of unemployment. This must be remedied.

Community groups have insufficient input into local government, especially in terms of functions that really matter (*e.g.* housing).

The government's claim to be promoting partnership is spurious — they are using funds to divide communities, providing inadequate information, rarely engaging in consultation.

A problem people in this area have to come to terms with is in-fighting among community groups, which should be avoided.

Class issues are often disguised. For example, professional, middle class people sometimes control community groups and make a good living out of it. Professional women working on issues of women's poverty are an example, as are many of the religious working in the community.

### Responses

Before doing anything else, the divided nature of the communities in question must be recognised — there are many conflicting interests.

A common issue which could be focused on is the common causes of marginalisation and powerlessness in communities.

A good first step would be more exchange of information between groups.

There has been a decline in the use of 'militant' action among community groups, in favour of a more compromise-oriented strategy based on negotiation (*e.g.* with government). We need to work out what that means and whether it is good or bad.

# 13. Media

*Peadar Kirby*

While one comes across some awful rags in the Third World, it is also true to say that the print media there can provide a breadth of viewpoints and of analysis which is very refreshing. This contrasts with the rather narrow range of views considered acceptable in our English-language media. In this regard some Irish-language media are closer to the best of the Third World media in their ability to examine issues with a greater thoroughness and commitment.

One gets the impression that Third World media are more aware of their ideological standpoint and therefore clearer about what political objective it espouses. This, of course, leads to the sort of right-wing political crusading of Chile's *El Mercurio*, of Nicaragua's *La Prensa* and of Jamaica's *The Daily Gleaner*, all papers notorious for their determined opposition to progressive governments, untroubled by any need to get their facts right.

At its best, however, it has led to the development of independent progressive newspapers and magazines such as *Uno Mas Uno* in Mexico City, *Epoca* in Santiago, *Fodhla de Saõ Paulo* in Saõ Paulo or *Paginas* in Lima, all papers and magazines characterised by the thoroughness with which they seek to examine their societies and their commitment to a more socially progressive society. They have developed media which, while independent, can see themselves as part of the broad left and share that left's aspirations.

By contrast, the Irish print media often appear too willing to devote themselves to the peripheral and even the frivolous while neglecting a more thorough examination of the key issues facing our society. This is particularly true of coverage of Northern Ireland and of our failure at national development. In this regard, the media are too willing to limit themselves to reflecting the narrow consensus of our political leadership without challenging the sterility of that consensus. If the lack of clear-cut ideological debate in Irish society is due to our inability so far to come to terms with our colonial past, then the Irish media can be said to reflect that malaise rather accurately.

Apart from the mainstream media, what also characterises many Third World societies is their flourishing 'alternative' media. These are media developed by the marginalised to communicate their own experience and help reflect on it. Here the media used are those most appropriate to the situation, so that drama, music and story-telling can take their place alongside the print media, radio and video. While grassroots groups here are beginning to develop their own media, all too often these are seen simply as vehicles for information rather than as platforms for debate and analysis. Again this reflects the ideologically impoverished nature of Irish society.

Finally a word about the electronic media. Throughout the Third World radio has become perhaps the most popular of all media and at its best can reflect and help develop more critical stances. Television, perhaps due to the expense of the technology, seems almost entirely to mirror a US model whereas video is being widely used for conscientisation purposes.

## *Workshop Report*

### Sources of news and censorship

It is difficult to get sources of international news. We are dependent on the international media in relation to other states rather than having a good network of Irish correspondents. One result of censorship is a closed state. We cannot express points of view in relation to the closest conflict. The range of debate over the North has narrowed over the past twenty years as a result.

## 'Left' media

In other countries, such as France, there is a well-established left which gives financial support to a left media. The lack of left media is a reflection of the lack of a left establishment in Ireland. Regarding the belief held by some that there is a positive conspiracy within the media against progressive forces, the argument was that there is not. However, it was argued, the media is not a repository of virtue as it both reflects and creates society. Resources are the key to being able to bombard the media. There is no substantial nationalist section of the bourgeoisie or there is no powerful interest group prepared to sponsor a radical paper. The state interferes directly relatively little. Advertising is all important. Rather than selling advertisements to readers a more correct analysis of the relationship is that readers are sold to advertisers. Market surveys are hugely important and developments are stringently based on their results. One major lesson newspapers have learnt from these surveys is that people do not want news. Thus news has suffered a lot relative to features.

## Local media

There is a total Dublin bias in the media and community radio is commercially dominated. Local papers are a thriving sector but there is a real vacuum in the area of magazines. Good investigative journalism in such a medium pushes issues into the general media.

## Partition

More than anything else the media is partitioned and as a result it reinforces partition. RTE is not at all conscious of listeners in Northern Ireland.

## Impartiality

The media reflect the rulers of society. 'Facts' are never value-free. All newspapers have an editorial policy. For example the *Irish Times* tries to stimulate a greater sense of the wider European identity. These values are communicated through omissions as well as through inclusions.

## Máss Culture

The bombardment of outside news and mass culture with no reference to Ireland blocks Irish society from creating itself. As a result of being English-speaking our media follow the Anglo-American model, thus ignoring the European tradition.

# 14. Multinationals

## Case study of pharmaceutical industry
*Vincent Tucker*

Since the late 1950s Ireland has adopted an export-oriented free market strategy of the kind which international bodies such as the International Monetary Fund and World Bank have been encouraging, and in some cases forcing, developing countries to adopt. This has involved a policy of integration into the international economy through removing protectionist measures and welcoming foreign investment, usually in the form of transnational corporations. This policy also involves relying mainly on free market forces and private enterprise, rather than state directed or controlled policies to make the investment decisions which shape development policy.

In this paper I want to concentrate on one sector of Irish development, the pharmaceutical industry. The growth of this industry is based on profit maximisation strategies which include overseas expansion creating new markets in the Third World, the proliferation of vast numbers of new drugs most of which (75 per cent according to most informed sources) are useless or in some cases dangerous, and intensive promotion in order to sell these drugs.

While the industry has undoubtedly made some major contributions to health care, most of what it now produces is of little or no therapeutic value. By the late 1960s other aspects of the industry had also come under scrutiny. The Sainsbury Committee in the UK and Senate sub-committee hearings in the U.S. revealed 'profiteering, price-fixing, promotion of ineffective drugs, questionable advertising and sales techniques, monopoly trading and suppression of information' (Chetley, 1990, 22). As it came under increasing scrutiny the industry chose to refer to itself as the 'health care industry' to promote the illusion that it is at the service of promoting better health. The reality is that in many instances the practices of the pharmaceutical industry have served to seriously distort health priorities. Drugs which are banned or restricted in parts of Europe and the US continue to be marketed in developing countries.

Ireland's relationship with the transnational pharmaceutical industry is a classic illustration of dependency — an unhealthy dependency. Dependency is the situation in which the form and structure of the development of a region or country is dictated by outside interests in a manner which is detrimental to the people of that country or to sectors of the population.

Ireland offered a number of attractions to the chemical and pharmaceutical industry. It provided access to EC markets as well as a place to locate a stage of production, bulk chemicals, formulation, or packaging and distribution functions, in a low or zero tax zone so as to create scope for transfer pricing. Ireland offered the lowest taxes on profits in Europe (0-10 per cent). This extremely low taxation policy is combined with double taxation agreements with a number of other countries. This makes Ireland, together with Puerto Rico, an important international platform for transfer pricing arrangements. The IDA played, and continues to play a very important role in promoting the development of the chemical and pharmaceutical industry in Ireland. As well as providing very substantial grants, the IDA has paved the way for the industry's expansion even in ways which infringe the rights of communities and citizens. The IDA played a major role, for example, in lobbying government so as to dissuade it from requiring companies to disclose financial data which they feared could be used, among others, by trade unionists campaigning for higher wages (Scrip 1985, 31). Unlike the Puerto Rican authorities the IDA was lax in monitoring company performance in terms of job creation or other economic indicators.

The benefits to the Irish economy have been described as 'minimal' by one economist, who carried out a detailed economic assessment of the industry (O Súilleabháin, 1983). Total employment is estimated by the IDA to be about 12,000 with about 6,700 of these employed in the pharmaceutical sector. Since the companies trade almost exclusively with their own subsidiaries, inward linkages to the Irish economy are also minimal — 3 per cent. Clearly what is good for the industry is not necessarily good for Ireland.

The influx of chemical and pharmaceutical companies to Ireland dates from the early 1970s at a time when the U.S. Environmental Protection Agency began to tighten its controls on the industry. In the U.S. companies pay 12 per cent of their profits on environmental costs whereas in Ireland they pay only 6 per cent. Ireland had neither the legislation nor the capacity to monitor the companies. Following an industrial development policy which almost indiscriminately welcomed all comers it did not wish to put any obstacles in the way of industries wishing to set up here. Concerned communities and environmentalists were offered company propaganda in place of proper controls and monitoring of the industry. However, various community actions and individual campaigns have been undertaken, *e.g.* John Hanrahan, a Tipperary farmer, won a Supreme Court case against Merck, Sharp and Dohme for serious damage to the health of his family and farm animals. Another campaign resulted in Merrell Dow cancelling their plans to establish a factory in a green belt area in Cork. A further outcome is that the government has been forced to enact some limited protective legislation. In the campaign against Sandoz, which resulted in a public hearing and widespread public debate, community groups won another important victory, and set a new European precedent by winning a community's right of access to company monitoring data.

When all these considerations are added to the balance sheet serious questions must be asked as to the appropriateness of encouraging the pharmaceutical industry as a major sector in Irish industrial development.

Is it not possible for Ireland to have its own pharmaceutical industry which could supply most of the needs of the General Medical Services at a considerable saving? One Irish company produced generic versions of 23 of the 30 most widely used drugs in the NHS at a fraction of the cost charged for the same drugs by the international companies. One might well ask why the GMS continues to import its drugs from the major companies at a price substantially greater than that charged to the UK government. The case of Bangladesh is instructive here.

In 1982 the Bangladesh government decided to set up its own drug industry to produce essential drugs cheaply and also banned 1,700 drugs as 'useless', non-essential and/or harmful (Chetley, 1990: 99). The transnational pharmaceutical industry reacted strongly in an attempt to squash this initiative. The industry summoned the support of the governments of the countries which were the largest producers of pharmaceuticals and exerted considerable pressure on the Bangladesh government to reverse its new drug policy. The U.S. and Germany threatened to withdraw their companies and ban all further industrial investment in the country. For the same reason, were the Department of Health to decide to purchase generic drugs at considerably cheaper rates this would be seen as a threat to the policies of the Department of Industry and Commerce who are anxious to woo even more companies to establish subsidiaries here.

However, various non-governmental organisations (NGOs) working at international level, as well as national organisations and community groups working at local level, have had considerable success in challenging the industry and asserting their rights. Here in Ireland campaigns by local community groups concerned with environmental health, in alliance with groups such as Greenpeace, have forced government, the IDA and industry to modify their policies. They have also engaged in the search for and promotion of alternatives. Ireland's reputation as a 'green' and relatively pollution-free country can be a major asset in taking advantage of the demand for chemical-free food in Europe.

The chemical/pharmaceutical industry has a negative impact on other forms of industry such as farming, food production, fishing and tourism. Where the IDA has attempted to foist industries on communities this has also resulted in a form of social pollution whereby bitter splits are caused within communities. When environmental damage, dangers to public health and the health of workers are added to these considerations, it would appear that the chemical and pharmaceutical industry is an unsuitable choice for Ireland.

We have something to learn from those countries which are more selective about the industries they support. Other late-industrialising countries have not been as indiscriminate as Ireland in welcoming all-comers. In Ireland development policy has been dictated by a rather naive laissez faire ideology. The dominance of this ideology among policy makers and economists has led to other alternatives being summarily dismissed as 'unrealistic'. It is essential therefore that we have a more open and wide-ranging debate as to what form of development and what forms of industrialisation are most appropriate for our particular needs.

# Lessons from Bhopal
## *Jim O'Neill*

Before turning to the Bhopal tragedy it would be useful to give an overview of multinational investment in both the North and South of Ireland and examine the similarities in investment policies between here and the developing world.

As R. Allen and T. Jones pointed out in *Guests of the Nation*, multinationals choose Ireland as a manufacturing base because of high productivity, labour flexibility, low labour costs, low or non-existent taxation, political stability (although not necessarily applicable to the North) and a highly attractive package of government-funded incentives.

One of the vehicles for these incentives has been the growth of Enterprise Zones or Free Trade Zones as they are known in the Third World. They provide a whole range of incentives, including exemption from rates and property taxes, which are offered to attract private investment and create employment. Ironically the first Free Trade Zone was set up at Shannon. As Marcel Barag pointed out, 'Since the creation of the first Free Trade Zone in Ireland in 1958 the élite of developing countries have created hundreds of other tax-free zones in agreement with multinationals. Foreign investors benefit from subsidised infrastructure, total freedom to repatriate profits and tax exemptions.'

Thus a concept which was borrowed from Ireland by developing countries has now been applied back to this country in the form of enterprise zones. Firms such as Du Pont, Molins and Courtaulds have been attracted to Derry by a skilled, relatively cheap labour force and financial incentives. Yet most of the multinationals pulled out either because the economic climate was no longer suitable or because the grants had run out. The only big multinational company that remains is Du Pont which has been in Derry since the late 1950s.

A particular attraction for chemical multinationals in Ireland has been the lack of adequate safety and environmental regulations in comparison with environmental protection laws in the U.S.. In Northern Ireland, for example, environmental protection is much less highly developed than in the rest of the U.K..

Thus while criticism is levelled at developing countries for their lax safety and environmental laws which encourage firms with hazardous technologies to invest there, the same criticism could be levelled at Ireland, where in the South particularly there has been a vast expansion of the chemical and pharmaceutical industry over the last two decades.

The deadly cloud of methyl isocyanate gas that overcame Bhopal on December 3rd, 1984 claimed over 2,000 lives and decimated tens of thousands of families. Yet as Anwar Fazal of the International Organisation of Consumer Unions pointed out, the aftermath of Bhopal would not only be remembered for being the world's worst ever industrial disaster but also for three other reasons (Martin Abraham, *The Lessons of Bhopal*).

1. It was just one of many industrial accidents that are becoming increasingly common in the rapidly industrialising Third World.

2. It was a mere symptom of a deeply rooted dependence on violent technologies that are devastatingly costly in terms of their impact on human lives.

3. It was a stark example of another gross failure of big technologies, big businesses and big government.

The same points could easily be applied here. It can be applied to the issues surrounding the present campaign against the toxic waste incinerator in Derry where chemical companies such as Du Pont see the incineration of hazardous wastes as the only 'safe' and 'reliable' method of its disposal. Yet experiences and research have shown that this method is anything but safe and reliable, with the effect on peoples' health and the surrounding environment proving to be devastating.

Therefore what lessons can be learnt from the disaster of Bhopal that could be applied to our own situation here? Parisar, an Indian environmental group which issued a statement on the lessons of Bhopal a year after the tragedy, best explains what could and should be done to avoid any similar type of disaster.

The Bhopal tragedy (and other similar industrial disasters the world over in the recent past) could have been averted if responsible representative people's organisations had access to the relevant information, as well as the legal authority to intervene in the situation as the Union Carbide Bhopal plant. For a long time secrecy and non-access to information and data have protected the "anti-people" activities of the vested interests within the industrial business world and the bureaucratic machinery of the government. All across the world events have repeatedly shown that governments by themselves have proved inadequate to intervene in time to prevent ecological disasters. Help must actively be sought from those sections of society whose lives and health are directly in danger, as well as from those who have a long-term scientific or cultural interest in "Spaceship Earth" *viz* naturalists, biologists, ecologists, historians, artists, *etc.* should by law be given the legal status and power as members of the inspecting authority through accredited representative bodies.

Various campaign groups in Ireland have continually fought for free access to information from the various multinational companies in their areas, but to little avail. The way that Du Pont in Derry has handled the issue of the toxic wast incinerator with local groups is symptomatic of that experience. Instead of giving access to the relevant information in a spirit of free and open debate, the company has engaged in a public relations exercise which attempts to put forward a positive corporate image. Hence we get bland statements about Du Pont's wonderful health and safety record and a warning about the uninformed hysteria that is being put about on the subject of toxic waste incineration.

Perhaps a policy statement from the International Organisation for Consumers Unions on the lessons of Bhopal best sums it up:

> But perhaps most important of all, international organisations must instil in both donor and recipient countries the notion that neither human health and safety nor environmental quality should  be sacrificed in the name of economic growth and national development.

That statement could just as easily be applied to multinational companies operating here in Ireland.

## Workshop Report

Some of the items of discussion were as follows:

* The huge power of multinational companies to influence govern-ments and international bodies (including lobbying and bribing) makes it difficult for people to challenge them. Apart from infor-mation-sharing, the possibilities for protest action at a collective, international level are limited.

* However, some useful international networks do good work in this area, *e.g.* the U.N. Centre for Transnational Companies collects useful data, and the Health Action Network links up groups and co-ordinates relevant campaigns (especially in terms of trying to create/change World Health Organisation directives).

* There are quite sophisticated environmental and safety standards in Ireland (and in many developing countries): the problem is that they are not enforced. Some of these come from the EC — this might allow action on the part of groups in terms of monitoring government behaviour (North and South) and reporting it to the EC.

* Some of the safeguards are being made outdated by new techno-logical developments (*e.g.* in the field of biotechnology) which are very difficult to respond to at a grassroots level. More information is needed in this area.

* Trade unions could do more and be less supportive, for example, of chemical companies locating here. They could initiate and run international campaigns, learning lessons from Third World and other countries. In fact, they are one of the few organisations which could do so.

*Abdullah Osman El-Tom*

# 15. Plenary

## On the Concept of 'Third World'
### *Abdullah Osman El-Tom*

It is obvious that many participants here are not satisfied with the use of the term 'third world'. The term itself originated in the French Revolution but became more popular after the Afro-Asian Bandung (Indonesia) Conference of 1955.

Though the term is expressive, it suffers the limitation of combining a large number of diverse countries. Recently the term 'fourth world' has been coined in addition to the terms 'first', 'second' and 'third world' to refer to the neglected poor in the industrialised world. If we are to avoid the use of this term for this conference, what are the other options available to us?

In the Brandt Report, the world is divided into North and South. The South refers to the poorest half of the world, the North to the rich. Like the term 'third world', North and South are supposed to be passive concepts free from any connotation of a structural link between the two sides of the world. This is despite the fact that the main contribution of the Brandt Report is based on the outcome of the structural relationship between North and South.

Many scholars still prefer to use the term 'poor/rich' in classifying different countries. The term 'poor' is normally used to relate the poverty of the Third World countries to their poor natural endowment. The problem to be faced here is that many of the supposedly poor countries are not really poor. Moreover, many of the countries currently classified as rich are naturally poor. If we are to emphasise the natural endowment of different countries, neither Japan nor Switzerland will fit their category well. The same thing could be said about many countries which are now classified as poor, like Nigeria, Egypt and Zimbabwe.

The terms 'developed' and 'developing' are occasionally used for the same purpose. Yet, it is a fact that many of the Third World countries cannot be correctly described as developing. On the contrary, they are, indeed, going backward. Moreover, the assumption that Western countries have all attained development is not altogether satisfactory.

The term 'underdeveloped' has also come into use for describing Third World countries. Unlike the terms, 'third/first world', 'south/north', this term is not passive. The term implies a structural relationship between the developed and the undeveloped world, a relationship in which development is seen as causally related to underdevelopment. Conservative elements in the West normally shy away from the use of this term as indicative of their refusal to take responsibility for the underdevelopment of the Third World. You might recall that neither Reagan nor Thatcher — nor, for that matter, Bush or Major — would use this term in their speeches. Due to the fact that we are interested in attracting a wide range of audience to this conference, I think that the use of the term underdevelopment might be counterproductive.

Despite the limitations of the term 'third world', I feel that its use for a conference like this is appropriate.

## *Plenary Report*

1. We Irish are struggling with a problem of identity, asking ourselves what does it mean to be Irish? Do we view ourselves as one cohesive group or as many diverse groups? In the past being Irish had a restrictive, sectarian definition. How could a Protestant be truly Irish, and how could a person be both Irish and gay? Travellers, ethnically different, could not be part of our society, and women were ignored. We need to build a less narrow, more pluralist, more tolerant society, which embraces minorities, so that no person or group can be excluded from citizenship, from participation in decision-making, from identifying individually and collectively as Irish.

We need to guard against creating divisions within our nation, a grim scenario where there are those with credentials, and others who are marginalised. The danger exists that in the flow of history the victimised natives can become the oppressor settlers. Ireland needs holistic development 'the freedom to explore and define ourselves within an Irish context'. We can use to our advantage insights from other development models (Scandinavia, Cuba) where we may adopt some admirable aspects of a system, such as equitable distribution of resources, and reject other features, such as the ignoring of human rights.

2. Our struggle to define, to identify who we are becomes clearer on recognition of the psychological boundaries we set ourselves. We, as inheritors of colonialism, need to exorcise the internalised and unconscious value systems we have adopted. Workers in community groups have firstly to deal with an inferiority complex in our national psyche, with lacking the self-confidence to challenge existing ways, with overcoming the fear of failure. We survive on small victories, by recognising that change is a long-term struggle, on solidarity with like-minded groups, on not giving up.

3. The boundaries in our psychological make-up are also political, arising in the question, where does our nation begin and end? Ironically, as we merge with Europe, our own unity on this island is unresolved. Developed nations have no problem with outspoken national pride and national assertiveness. We, however, have difficulty in acknowledging and celebrating our origins, as the official embarrassment and equivocating during the recent 1916 commemorations showed.

4. Ironically, as world leaders are validating the emerging nationalism of Eastern Europe, USSR and the Balkans, to be nationalist in Ireland is suspect, even seditious, certainly linked with violence. The increasing illegitimacy of nationalism is on two levels. On the one hand at the conscious level, we fear contamination from the North, violence spilling over to the South, leading to the break-up of our structures, and the flight of foreign investment CRD must acknowledge this fear, must take it into account, must continue to get people to discuss issues in a North/South context, and must make links appear less threatening.

On the other hand at an unconscious level, people grew up here with partition as a given, the 26 counties as a *fait accompli*. Hence it takes a leap of the imagination to bracket together the two parts of the island, to perceive the relevance of linking, and to develop connections between groups working on common issues. In short, we should begin to recognise that we have problems in common and that it is in our best interests to solve these jointly. Events such as today's show there is a fund of goodwill and understanding on which to build.